Something to Talk About

Occasions We Celebrate in South Louisiana

Junior League of Lafayette, Louisiana

Something
to Talk About

Occasions We Celebrate in South Louisiana

Junior League of Lafayette, Louisiana

Something to Talk About
Occasions We Celebrate in South Louisiana

Published by the Junior League of Lafayette, Inc.

Copyright © 2005 by
Junior League of Lafayette, Inc.
504 Richland Avenue
Lafayette, Louisiana 70508
337.988.2739

www.juniorleagueoflafayette.com

Something to Talk About—Occasions We Celebrate in South Louisiana
is a collection of favorite recipes, which are not necessarily original recipes.

Library of Congress Catalog Number: 2005927581
ISBN: 0-935032-51-7

Photography: © Paul Rico
Food Styling: Sandra Day

Edited, Designed, and Manufactured by
Favorite Recipes® Press
An imprint of

FRP

P. O. Box 305142
Nashville, Tennessee 37230
800.358.0560

Art Director: Steve Newman
Book Design: Starletta Polster
Project Editor: Linda A. Jones

Manufactured in the United States of America
First Printing: 2005
40,000 copies

Something to Talk About
Development Committee

Michelle Curtis—*Chair*
Miriam Bourgeois—*Sustaining Advisor*

Anne Black—*Kitchen Testing Coordinator*
Katherine McDonald Bourg—*Recipe Coordinator*
Mary Michael Butcher—*Art & Design Coordinator*
Charlotte Cryer—*Recipe Coordinator*
Ann Morehead Marino—*Text/Nonrecipe Coordinator*
Allison Womble—*Recipe Coordinator*

Something to Talk About
Advisory Committee

Judy Mahtook—*Chair*

Amy Aderman	Laura Ann Edwards	Faith Moody
Sarah Beacham	Mimi Francez	Angela Morrison
Janet Begneaud	Ormond Guenard	Cecile Mouton
Miriam Bourgeois	Julie Hill	Julie Nelson
Ellen Cook	Betsy Koke	Stacy Patin
Michelle Curtis	Miriam Kolwe	Anne Sagrera
Rhonda Darby	Janice LeBlanc	Jeigh Stipe
Deborah D. Eckholdt	Marilyn Lee	Dana Topham

Executive Leadership

2003–2004 President—Marilyn Lee
2004–2005 President—Faith Moody
2005–2006 President—Angela Morrison

Credits

Photography—Paul Rico
Food Styling—Sandra Day

Special thanks to the University of Louisiana at Lafayette.

About the Junior League of Lafayette

The Junior League of Lafayette is an organization of women committed to promoting voluntarism, developing the potential of women, and improving the community through the effective action and leadership of trained volunteers. Its purpose is exclusively educational and charitable.

Since 1957, the Junior League of Lafayette has worked tirelessly toward the fulfillment of its above stated mission. Through innumerable hours of hands-on community voluntarism and the targeted distribution of financial resources, the trained volunteers of the Junior League of Lafayette have contributed to the positive and healthy development of generations of children. The Volunteer Center of Lafayette, The Family Tree Information, Education, and Counseling Center, and the Paul and Lulu Hilliard University Art Museum are but a few of the diverse organizations created or fostered by the efforts of the Junior League of Lafayette. Countless other nonprofit organizations have benefited from Junior League of Lafayette-assisted programs and from the distribution of grant monies. These efforts have positively affected the lives of our area's families and will hopefully leave a legacy of a richer, healthier, and more vibrant South Louisiana.

The Fleur-de-Lis

Originally a symbol of French royalty, the fleur-de-lis, or "flower of the lily," is a beloved reminder of South Louisiana's proud French heritage. The three-pronged fleur-de-lis makes its appearance on the Louisiana Acadiana flag and is the adopted symbol of many South Louisiana businesses, schools, and organizations. The Junior League of Lafayette has done the same, incorporating the symbol into its logo and using this identifiable symbol throughout this book.

Our Home

Where is South Louisiana? "South Louisiana" means different things to the different people using, and hearing, the term. Some consider it to be the southerly portion of Louisiana, reaching from the Mississippi border on the east to the Sabine River on the west. In a sense, this geographical designation is correct. However, those of us in Lafayette tend to use South Louisiana to describe the region surrounding our home—the multi-parish area referred to collectively as "Acadiana." The area is the adopted home of many of the "Acadians," French-speaking Catholics who migrated here after being forced from Acadie, present-day Nova Scotia, due to their refusal to swear loyalty to the British Crown. We are fiercely proud of this part of our heritage, and it is a common theme reflected in so many different facets of life in Acadiana. After all, we boast that this is the heart of "Cajun Country."

However, our story and history neither begin nor end with this legendary travail. Acadiana's world-renowned cuisine, artistic sensibilities, and other virtues are the result of many contributors to the region's cultural mix. Beginning with the area's Native American population, our home has filled with immigrants and settlers arriving from every corner of the world and by every circumstance imaginable. The varied surnames encountered in today's Acadiana are indicative of the countless nations and ethnicities now represented. Acadiana as we know and celebrate it bears the influence of all of these distinctive groups. Individually and collectively, these groups have made Acadiana what it is today. This is the South Louisiana we know and proudly display for all to see, sample, and enjoy.

Contents

Junior League of
Lafayette Publications 224

Introduction

Besides our famous food, what *do* we talk about in South Louisiana? We proudly talk about our area's famed Cajun heritage, captured in literature, song, and legend. We talk about the arts, apparent in our vibrant cultural scene, full of renowned musicians, first-rate museums, and talented artisans. We talk about South Louisiana's uniquely beautiful landscapes of cypress-filled bayous, reedy and wild marshes, golden rice fields, and live oaks laden with Spanish moss. We talk about South Louisianans' habit of celebrating each day to its fullest.

But without fail, we always talk about food. Even while enjoying one flavorful meal, our conversation often turns to fondly remembered meals of the past, or the anticipation of meals yet to come. This is with good reason, as South Louisiana is well known, and justifiably so, for the ingredients of our cuisine, the unique tastes prepared in our kitchens, the abundant feasts combining these tastes, and the social customs surrounding our cooking, feasting, and celebrating.

We are blessed with coastal waters and marshes that provide the ingredients for many of our most defining dishes. Cold, salty oysters are a given; some might say a birthright. And like their parents, even the youngest children quickly work through tables piled high with hot and spicy crawfish. Of course, we are not limited to the fruits of the waterways—many of our favorite meals feature beef, pork, venison, duck, or goose. This wealth of the South Louisiana pantry has created a region of discriminating palates. Meals that merely get the job done have no place on our tables. Everything must be seasoned to perfection and prepared just as our mothers and grandmothers did. More than one cross word has been exchanged over the appropriate thickness of gumbo! Whatever the dish, both home cooks and professional chefs alike expect fish straight from the Gulf, the choicest cuts of meat from trusted butchers, and the freshest of local fruits and vegetables. Undoubtedly, everyone has heard that South Louisiana food is spicy. It can be. Not for its own sake, though, but to enhance the rich and varied flavors of the other ingredients.

Many of our favorite dishes are well known, such as gumbo or jambalaya. But there are so many others dear to our hearts, such as Cajun Fried Turkey, Injected Pork Roast with Tangy Satsuma Sauce, Shrimp Grillades, and old-fashioned Marbled Syrup Cake. The list is blissfully endless.

However, celebrations in South Louisiana rarely end with the last course. It is no coincidence that some of our most popular restaurants feature live music and a dance floor that may be filled, even at breakfast, with adults and children moving to stirring Cajun or Zydeco tunes. Make no mistake, South Louisiana is not a tap-your-toes destination. No, it is a place to push back your chair and join the crowd on the dance floor.

With this Louisiana Gulf Coast love of life in mind, the Junior League of Lafayette proudly presents its newest collection of favorite regional recipes, *Something to Talk About—Occasions We Celebrate in South Louisiana*. We hope that you will turn the page, peruse a few of the menus from the celebrations of our lives—both large and small, formal and informal—and consider how you might re-create a little of South Louisiana's spirited lifestyle in your own neighborhood. The recipes that follow these twelve occasional menus continue in the tradition of our previous collections, *Talk About Good!* *Talk About Good II*, and *Tell Me More*, as they are the recipes of our own kitchens and those of our families and treasured friends. We hope that you will enjoy these recipes, combine them with your own family favorites, turn up the music, and, like us, celebrate all that the day has to offer.

Enjoy!

Occasional Menus

Bon
Appétit

Bon Appétit

The supper club—a popular excuse for couples to regularly enjoy one another's company. What better way to celebrate the monthly gathering than with a flavorful tribute to a favorite cuisine. From Spain to Greece, to the flavors of Tuscany, each hostess can research and taste-test until the menu accurately reflects her chosen region. The French menu, a South Louisiana favorite, recalls the region's famed French ties. Because the basic methods of preparation of our own Cajun cuisine hint at traditional French techniques, a return to a classically prepared French menu combines the familiar with a bit of Continental flair. Set the scene for an evening of warm and inviting brasserie fare—your guests will certainly approve!

Chez Vous. . .

The classic cheese course before dessert is a must. Consider a creamy Brie or Camembert, a bold and pungent Roquefort, or any number of delicious goat's milk cheeses, chèvre. Your local gourmet store can offer a wealth of information for creating the perfect balance of flavors and textures for your own cheese board.

What French meal is complete without a loaf of crusty bread? Although delicious alone, your guests will appreciate a bit of Normandy butter and that finishing touch, an individual salt cellar containing Fleur de Sel, a delicate Britton sea salt, perfect for a light dusting atop the butter.

The Kir Royale, a refreshing cocktail combining good quality Champagne and crème de cassis, is a popular choice for a French menu. Other options as an accompaniment to Coq au Vin include any number of red wines—perhaps a French burgundy, a côtes du Rhône or an American pinot noir.

Menu

L'apéritif
Kir Royale

L'entrée
Champignon Escargots

La salade verte
Salade Verte avec Vinaigrette

Le plat principal
Coq au Vin

Le fromage
Camembert and Brie

Le dessert
Tarte Tatin

Join the Krewe

Join the Krewe

Mardi Gras is associated with excess and a day for which Louisiana has become famous. In South Louisiana, however, the day is largely family-oriented and less of a ribald affair than one might expect. The day begins with a parade or two, hosted by local social organizations, or "krewes." Costumed and masked krewe members ride atop festive floats, throwing any number of trinkets to up-stretched hands, including commemorative coins, or doubloons, and the perennial favorite—beads. Those living near the parade route often host pre-parade breakfasts, so that guests might enjoy a decadent feast before heading en masse, and in lively spirits, to the parade.

When the parade rolls your way. . .

Decorate your Mardi Gras event with the colors of the day—purple, green, and gold. Colorful doubloons and strands of beads collected from years past are wonderful additions to any Mardi Gras table.

Every Mardi Gras celebration features a King Cake, a confection often adorned with purple, green, and gold sugars. Local bakeries offer their signature versions, creating a bit of rivalry among those preferring certain tastes. Some prefer a filled cake, perhaps fruit or cream cheese and pecan, while others argue that a simple, cinnamon-flavored cake is more traditional. Since King Cakes are widely available for shipping, you must sample a few to find your own favorite!

And to take away . . . Inexpensive cloth bags are perfect for your guests to carry to the parade to collect their "catch." Local printers can personalize your bags and emblazon them with your choice of wording and Mardi Gras design.

Menu

Beverage
Jester's Milk Punch

Appetizers
Carnival Crab Meat Dip
Pesto Feta Cheese Loaf

Salad
Frozen Fruit Salad

Entrées
King's Egg Casserole
Shrimp Grillades with
Jalapeño Cheese Grits

Bread
Royal Drop Biscuits

Desserts
Mardi Gras Coffee Cake
Cream Cheese Danish Squares

The Lenten Tradition

The Lenten Tradition

The excesses of Mardi Gras season do not last forever. Promptly at midnight, Mardi Gras gives way to Lent with the arrival of Ash Wednesday. Perhaps due to its large Catholic population, South Louisiana remains steadfast in its observation of Lent, an observation continuing until Easter Sunday. Fish, shellfish, and vegetable-based selections are featured on local restaurant menus, as many residents abstain from meat in their Friday dining choices. In area homes, Lent is often observed with a Friday evening fish fry or seafood boil. These warm, casual gatherings allow hosts and guests alike to contribute, whether that contribution is the location, the fish, the extras, or time-tested expertise in providing the perfect blend of spices.

On Fridays in your home. . .

Whether a coating of cornmeal, flour, or bread crumbs (maybe even a pecan-meal crust), every South Louisiana chef has a favorite fish-fry blend. Perhaps you like a bit of beer in your batter or a little heat in the mix. However, it is hard to go wrong with fresh fish, nice weather, and a gathering of good friends.

*And while the oil is hot. . .*add a little something extra, a bit of lagniappe if you will. The extras make the meal and personalize the gathering. Why not add potatoes, favorite hush puppies, or a few breaded vegetables?

A seafood boil you say? Everyone is a chef, of course, so let your guests prepare cocktail sauce to their own taste. They will appreciate an individual ramekin and the classic ingredients—ketchup, chili sauce, prepared horseradish, Worcestershire sauce, mayonnaise, and lemon wedges.

Menu

Beverage
Pitcher Perfect Lemonade

Appetizers
Black Bean Salsa
Layered Seafood Dip
Two-Tomato Tapas

Salad
Colorful Coleslaw

Entrée
Deep-Fried Fish

Bread
Jalapeño Hush Puppies

Sides
Carrot Beignets
Fried Mushrooms and Fried Zucchini
Green Beans and Potatoes

Desserts
Chocolate Chip Bundt Cake
Awesome Oatmeal Cookies

A Table for Two

A Table for Two

When celebrating a particularly special day—perhaps your wedding anniversary—a boisterous restaurant may not do. Observing the evening at home presents an opportunity to prepare a new recipe, set your table creatively with your finest, or simply treat that special someone to a pampered evening. The menu should be filled with favorite tastes, but try preparing them in an innovative style. The time it takes to prepare the meal will quickly be forgotten after the first delicious course and a few sips of Champagne. With the telephone off the hook and the children at the sitter's, the quiet and intimate home setting lets you leave the busy work-week at the office (for the evening, anyway!).

At your own table for two. . .

Make it a joint effort. No need to shoulder the preparation alone—shared slicing and dicing duties can become a part of the evening. With a cocktail-hour glass of Champagne, even the most kitchen-averse spouse will be eager to offer a bit of culinary assistance.

Indulge. Consider hiring a personal chef or catering firm for the day to take care of the tedious details. Your chef can use your recipes or bring her own, adapting them to your tastes. You are left with fully prepared dishes, allowing you to enjoy the best of going out and staying in.

For me? Present your beautifully wrapped gem of an anniversary gift atop your spouse's place setting. This can be a generous start to a sparkling evening.

Menu

Beverage
Champagne

Appetizer
Shrimp Relish

Entrée
Grilled Salmon
with Homemade Dill Mayonnaise

Sides
Broiled Stuffed Tomatoes
Creamy Lemon Rice

Desserts
Kahlúa Pecan Fudge Pie
Chocolate-Dipped Strawberries

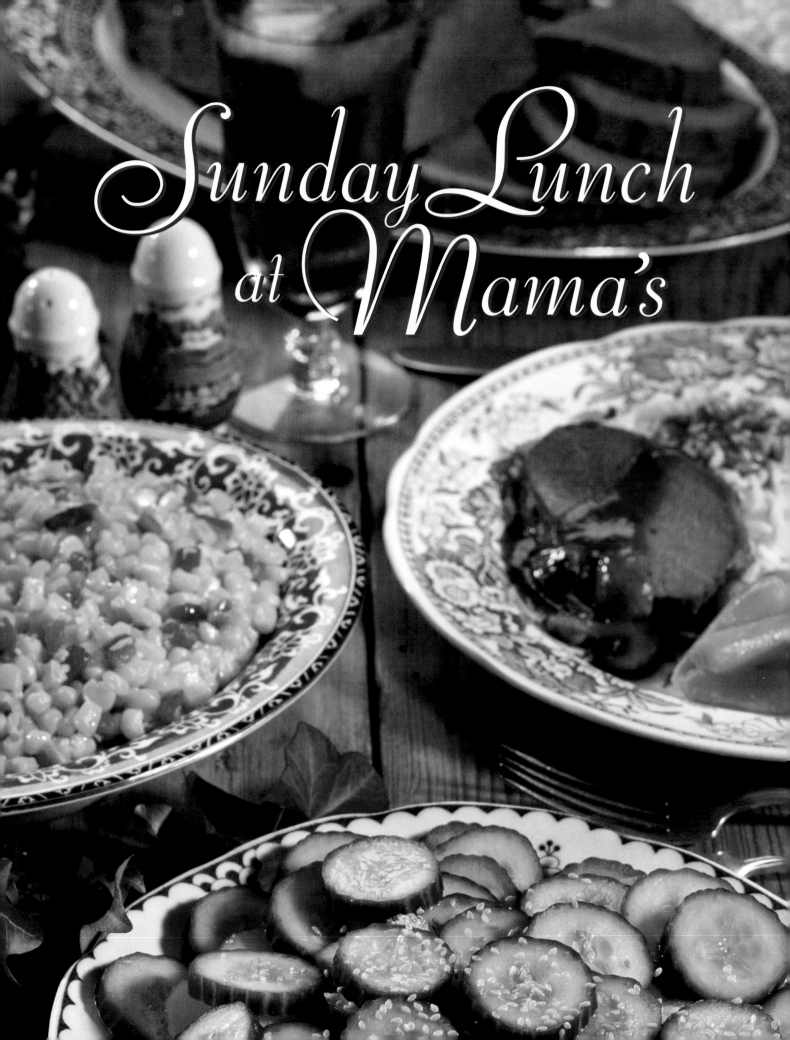

Sunday Lunch at Mama's

Sunday Lunch at Mama's

No invitation is necessary, no phone calls need be made. Simply put, those in South Louisiana know where they will enjoy Sunday lunch—with the family. This type of weekly gathering is one evoking the fondest memories of hearth and home. What's on the menu? No surprises in the repertoire here, the table is set with dishes that have been on the family's menu for generations. While a "nouveau" item or two may be appropriate elsewhere, there is little intention of changing the familiar Sunday meal. Featuring tender, slow-cooked roasts, rice and gravy prepared to the family's taste, a few hearty vegetables, and always a tempting dessert, or two, these easygoing Sunday feasts are a perfect end to the week.

For Sunday afternoon with your family. . .

Learning your lesson. Grandmothers, mothers, and aunts have decades of kitchen advice to share. Family get-togethers offer an opportunity to pass that experience along. Ask questions, listen, and observe. Soon, new generations will be asking for your advice.

The group is together—what a perfect time to take care of those time-consuming kitchen chores. Whether canning the summer's harvest, making fig preserves, or shelling beans, the warm and familiar conversation is certain to make these after-lunch tasks effortless.

Do you have the recipe for. . . ? Mothers and grandmothers have heard the question countless times. New, user-friendly computer programs have simplified the task of compiling the family's favorites. Once completed, printed versions of the newly compiled family cookbook make wonderful presents.

Menu

Salad
Sweet-and-Sour Cucumber Salad

Entrées
Sunday Roast with Rice and Gravy
Shrimp, Crab Meat and Eggplant Casserole

Bread
Spinach Cheese Loaf

Sides
Tomato Pie
Corn Maque Choux
Carrots in Orange Sauce

Dessert
Marbled Syrup Cake

The Bridal Party

The Bridal Party

Hosting an elegant pre-wedding gathering of the bride-to-be's closest friends is a generous gesture. The bridesmaids' luncheon is often one of a South Louisiana bride's most anticipated events, a time to enjoy a few memories and cheerful conversations before the biggest of days. Although every hostess has her preferences for making the day perfect, a few items are a given for such a splendid affair—light libations, menu selections with a feminine flair, and, most certainly, an abundance of the season's most exquisite flowers. Raise a glass, ladies, and offer a toast to treasured friends and hopeful beginnings.

For your own bride. . .

Only the finest will do. Polish the heirloom silver until gleaming, press the linens until crisp, and arrange the hand-lettered place cards with precision. Yes, such a gathering requires much thought and preparation, but your efforts will be noticed in the flawless details and will create lasting memories of a day executed to perfection.

Create a unique centerpiece. Consider arranging your garden's most beautiful blooms in a vintage beaded handbag, a sterling ice bucket, or an antique teapot. Perhaps some of your more delicate blossoms could be included in individual nosegays for placement before each guest's table setting.

A generous touch. Arrange for a small gift bag for the bride and her bridesmaids. Bags might contain a few items for the wedding day—a carefully chosen lip balm, a pale nail polish, a disposable camera, or a few beautifully wrapped pre-wedding sweets.

Menu

Beverages
Bellinis
Iced Cappuccino

Appetizers
Cheese and Pecan Stars
Spinach and Artichoke Pinwheels

Soup
Corn and Crawfish Bisque

Salad
Fruity Spring Mix Salad with
Sweet and Hot Vinaigrette
and Poppy Seed Puff Pastry Straws

Dessert
Chocolate Amaretto Tarts

A Flavorful Fourth

A Flavorful Fourth

The backyard Independence Day celebration is an American tradition. Although the weather sizzles in July, South Louisiana shares in that tradition, doing so poolside, on the deck, or at the family camp. It is the kind of laugh-out-loud, barefoot gathering where everyone is welcome—including the dog. With jabbering children, a note or two of Zydeco or Swamp-Pop music in the air, and good-natured banter among the adults, it seems that the menu could take a backseat on such a day, but not so as South Louisiana offers an abundance of seasonal, warm-weather choices to entice the party-goers. Bring out those vine-ripe July tomatoes, slice that icy-cold watermelon, savor the spicy selections from the grill, and anticipate the fireworks to come.

In your own backyard. . .

Before July brings the berry season to a close in Louisiana, families trek to berry farms, picking blueberries from the vine. Louisiana berries are wonderfully plump and sweet—perfect for pies, preserves, hand-cranked ice creams, and any number of summertime favorites.

Keep it local. With microbreweries appearing on corners everywhere, it is easy to give your guests a selection of regional bottled beer to accompany their backyard meal. An inexpensive galvanized tub, chilled to perfection with a selection of local brews, is hard to resist. A second tub, containing iced bottles of nonalcoholic selections, is a tempting alternative.

The uninvited guests. Purchase a few inexpensive citronella tiki torches to keep mosquitoes at bay. Your guests will also appreciate a selection of bug sprays and creams in case the party goes a bit later than planned.

Menu

Beverage
Red Rooster

Appetizers
Cilantro Salsa
Bacon, Lettuce and Tomato Dip

Salads
Grape Salad
Jambalaya Salad

Entrées
Beef Brisket "To Die For"
Chili Lime Chicken Kabobs

Bread
California Artichoke Bread

Sides
Calico Beans
Vidalia Onion Pie
Hash Brown Casserole

Desserts
Peanut Butter Cups
Chocolate Chip Pecan Pie Bars
Strawberry and Blueberry Trifle

Cher Bébé

Cher Bébé

"Cher bébé" is a South Louisiana expression of the warmest kind—one heard as friends and passersby greet a family's new addition. Perhaps that introduction is made at the newborn's first "public" event, the Sip & See. A modern approach to the traditional baby shower, the Sip & See allows a new mother to proudly present her bundle of joy to an extended group of friends, without having to do so in her own home, preserving her much-needed energy for tending to her growing family's busy schedule. Guests enjoy conversation, a few delicious nibbles, a cup of punch, and perhaps extend a few words of wisdom for the days ahead. With one final glance and a much admiring "cher bébé," the guests are on their way.

For your own welcome additions. . .

Consider a teatime affair. While a Sip & See is not limited to a particular time of day, offerings at teatime are light, delicate, and perfect for those who might drop by for a quick word.

The hostess's table must be abundant, piled high with seasonal fruits and laden with trays of tempting tea sandwiches and bite-sized sweets. No such table is complete without a selection of petits fours, a delicate and time-consuming treat best enjoyed when purchased from your favorite baker and placed alongside your own home-baked offerings.

Do I bring a gift? While the gift option should be left to the new mother, the Sip & See is not for stocking the baby's nursery, as the traditional shower has been, but is, instead, an opportunity for the new mother to easily introduce the new baby to her friends.

Menu

Beverages
Southern Belle Punch
Spiced Tea

Sandwiches
English Cucumber Sandwiches
Baked Cheese Petits Fours
Roasted Chicken Salad Sandwiches

Dips
Fruit and Yogurt Dip
Cold Shrimp Dip

Sweets
Dark Chocolate Cookies
Scotch Shortbread
Lemon Curd Tarts
Cinnamon Logs

The Pre-Game Show

The Pre-Game Show

Once a practical place to snack before attending the game, the tailgate party has become an event unto itself. Gone are the days of cheese and crackers. Today's pre-game party provides every sports-loving chef with a weekly opportunity to impress fellow fans with treats tailor-made for an all-day, raucous gathering. In South Louisiana, home of Louisiana's Ragin' Cajuns®, the tailgating menu focuses on well-loved staples—jambalaya, gumbos, and hearty snack foods. While some prefer to complete their cooking at home, others invest in portable cooktops, heavy-duty grills, and any number of outdoor essentials for on-site preparation to better enjoy the camaraderie of fellow game-day chefs. Competition for the tastiest menu and most elaborate arrangement is, naturally, part of the experience.

For your own home games. . .

Necessities? Some hosts treat tailgating guests to a bit of luxury—heaters to warm the toes for the cool games, tents in the event of inclement weather, and, rain or shine, a television to keep track of the conference scores.

It is just a game, after all. No need to prepare everything on-site or even on your own. Combine your own creations with those from local caterers and restaurants—no one has to know. Just call ahead and pick up those platters on the way to the stadium.

No heavy lifting necessary. For large gatherings, contact local party rental businesses, which will often deliver and retrieve the basics for your tailgate—tables, tents, and maybe even the margarita machine.

Menu

Beverage
Cajun Bloody Marys

Appetizers
Mexican Dip
Feta Cheese Spread
Spinach Cheese Squares
Half Time Buffalo Wings

Salad
Marinated Shrimp Tortellini

Entrée
Jambalaya for a Crowd

Desserts
Touchdown Trail Mix
Pralines
Pecan Pie Brownies

Bounty of the Bayou

Bounty of the Bayou

While others enjoy beach houses, lakeside bungalows, or mountain cabins, those in South Louisiana retreat to their camps. Wherever its rural location, and whether affording a gulf view or a bayou vista, the camp is a year-round getaway, allowing access to any number of water sports and an opportunity to relax, cook, and enjoy a more leisurely lifestyle. But, when the air turns crisp, South Louisiana packs its collective gear for the camp, anticipating the arrival of the fall hunting seasons and the promise of the state's nickname—"Sportsman's Paradise." Hunters begin to look skyward for a variety of fowl, thinking of the flavorful gumbos to come, and to the state's waterways for the catch of the day. No need to order out; tonight we keep our catch!

Your own Sportsman's Paradise...

Fireside pastimes. Although the camp provides the modern amenities of home and any number of diversions, many spend the evening fireside, with a deck of cards and the occasional friendly wager. Bourré, a classic Cajun card game, is a traditional favorite.

The house blend. Every camp has a signature camp punch, always a festive concoction including a favorite liquor, or two, which has been perfected by camp members and enjoyed by its guests over the years.

Men reign in the camp kitchen, taking pride in their game-based creations and building an ever-increasing repertoire of camp-style recipes to share with their guests. Many of these hearty creations are slow-cooked in nature, requiring a bit of sampling and a bit of tweaking as the dish simmers away.

Menu

Beverage
Whiskey Slush

Appetizers
Pepper Jelly Cheese Dip
Crawfish Dip

Gumbo
Duck and Andouille Gumbo

Entrées
Mushroom Venison Roast
Smothered Doves
Oak Grove Oyster Pie

Side
Smothered Okra

Dessert
Coconut Bread Pudding

A Day of Thanks

A Day of Thanks

Thanksgiving—no occasion is more identified with tradition. Although observed throughout America, regional flavors weave their way into local celebrations. Thanksgiving tables in South Louisiana feature tastes specific to the season. With the arrival of autumn, many Acadiana favorites are fresh from the harvest—wonderfully sweet yams, meaty pecans, any number of local rice varieties, and rich, thick cane syrup. These local ingredients appear in dishes gracing the Thanksgiving table, as families and friends gather and reflect on lives abundant with blessings.

A touch of Louisiana on your table...

A fried turkey? Many now know what South Louisiana has known for years—a deep-fried turkey is deliciously moist, not greasy as one might suspect. Gear for the frying process is available from any number of Louisiana-based sources, ensuring an authentic, and safe, fried-turkey experience.

An extra bit of flavor. Meat and poultry choices take on a bright new Louisiana flavor with "injections" of a favorite marinade, whether store-bought or a seasoned blend of your own creation. Experiment until the mixture is to your taste, then inject the roast, loin, or bird prior to cooking by your preferred method. Injectors (imagine a large syringe) are now available throughout the country.

Consider a Louisiana showstopper—the turducken. Prepared by local butchers, many of whom ship their products, the turducken features boneless turkey, stuffed with boneless duck and chicken. Any number of flavorful stuffings are included between the layers, completing what is sure to be the center of attention.

Menu

Appetizers
Mushroom-Stuffed Brie
Cranberry Jalapeño Relish over Cream Cheese

Salad
Orange Sherbet Salad

Entrées
Cajun Fried Turkey
Injected Pork Roast with Tangy Satsuma Sauce

Bread
Parker House Rolls

Sides
Spinach la Louisiane
Sweet Potatoes au Gratin
Seafood Corn Bread Dressing
Oyster Rice Dressing

Desserts
Pumpkin Cheesecake with Gingersnap Crust
Red Delicious Apple Cake
Southern Pecan Tart

Christmas Kibbies & Cocktails

Christmas Kibbies & Cocktails

The richness of South Louisiana's food heritage does not stem solely from its well-known French roots. Rather, the area is a melting pot of numerous cultures, each contributing its unique customs and cuisine to the mix. How better to honor an identifiable food heritage than by presenting an array of its best-loved selections at a holiday cocktail party, where spirited conversation and a lively mix of acquaintances combine for an evening of good cheer. Our choice for the holiday gathering pairs tempting cocktails with menu selections from the area's Lebanese tradition. South Louisiana's fondness for Lebanese cuisine is reflected in some of its most popular restaurants and sought-after recipes. Those recipes, presented in an opulent setting, provide a foundation for a sparkling evening.

Your own soirée. . .

If serving dishes unfamiliar to your guests, a small menu card containing a brief description of the dish placed before each selection is a great help. Guests can confidently navigate the selections, deciding which new tastes to sample.

This menu's namesake hors d'ouevre, the Kibbi, is a favorite Lebanese dish, one combining ground lamb or beef with cracked wheat and seasonings. Our version is formed into football-shaped morsels and fried to provide a tasty cocktail accompaniment.

A bit of help. Preparing for a large-scale event can seem overwhelming for even the most seasoned of hostesses. For those time-consuming selections, such as Grape Leaves, why not invite a few friends or family members to a breakfast or coffee-hour gathering, where a few extra hands can assist in the preparation.

Menu

Beverages
Appletinis
Christmas Cosmopolitans

Appetizers
Grape Leaves
Hummus bi Tahini
Baba Ghanoush

Salad
Tabouli

Entrées
Fried Kibbies
Dripped Beef

Dessert
Baklava

Appetizers & Beverages

Mushroom-Stuffed Brie

2 tablespoons unsalted butter
1 small red onion, finely chopped
8 ounces portobello mushrooms,
    finely chopped
1 tablespoon dry sherry

1/2 teaspoon grated nutmeg
1 (17-ounce) package puff pastry sheets,
    thawed
1 (14-ounce) Brie round, chilled
1 egg, beaten

Preheat the oven to 425 degrees. Melt the butter in a large skillet over medium heat. Stir in the onion, mushrooms, sherry and nutmeg. Sauté until the vegetables are tender and the liquid is absorbed. Let cool. Roll 1 sheet of puff pastry into a 13-inch square on a lightly floured surface. Place the Brie on the pastry and cut a circle, leaving a 1-inch lip. Roll another sheet of puff pastry and cut a circle of the same size. Slice the Brie in half horizontally. Spread the mushroom mixture over the bottom half of the Brie and top with the upper half. Place 1 of the pastry circles on a baking sheet. Top with the Brie and fold the edges of the pastry up around the Brie. Top with the second circle of pastry and press the edges around the Brie to form a tight seal. Brush the pastry with the egg. Bake for 20 minutes. Let cool on a rack for 15 minutes before serving. Serve with crackers or bread.

SERVES 10 TO 12

Marinated Cheese

1/2 cup olive oil
1/2 cup white wine vinegar
1 (2-ounce) jar diced pimentos
3 tablespoons chopped fresh parsley
3 tablespoons minced green onions
3 garlic cloves, minced
1 teaspoon sugar

3/4 teaspoon dried basil
1/2 teaspoon salt
1/2 teaspoon pepper
8 ounces sharp Cheddar cheese,
    cut into 1-inch cubes
8 ounces cream cheese, cut into
    1-inch cubes

Combine the olive oil, vinegar, pimentos, parsley, green onions, garlic, sugar, basil, salt and pepper in a jar and shake well. Arrange the Cheddar cheese cubes and cream cheese cubes alternately in a serving dish. Pour the marinade over the cheese. Marinate in the refrigerator for at least 8 hours.

SERVES 6 TO 8

Shrimp-Stuffed Portobello Mushrooms

1/4 cup olive oil
1/2 cup chopped onion
1/4 cup chopped fresh basil
3 large garlic cloves, minced
1/2 teaspoon chopped fresh rosemary
6 ounces peeled cooked bay shrimp, or
    8 ounces lump crab meat
2/3 cup fresh bread crumbs

1/2 cup (2 ounces) grated
    Parmesan cheese
1/4 cup mayonnaise
1/2 teaspoon cayenne pepper
Salt and black pepper to taste
8 (2- to 2 1/2-inch) portobello
    mushrooms, gills removed

Preheat the oven to 350 degrees. Heat the olive oil in a large heavy skillet over medium-high heat. Stir in the onion, basil, garlic and rosemary. Sauté for 5 minutes or until the onion is tender. Remove to a bowl. Stir in the shrimp, bread crumbs, cheese, mayonnaise and cayenne pepper and mix well. Season with salt and black pepper. Arrange the mushrooms rounded side down on an oiled baking sheet. Mound the shrimp filling in the mushrooms, pressing gently to compact. Bake for 30 minutes or until the mushrooms are tender.

SERVES 4

Champignon Escargots

1 cup (2 sticks) unsalted butter
1/2 cup chopped fresh parsley
1 garlic clove, minced
1 teaspoon salt

1 teaspoon pepper
2 pounds button mushrooms, chopped
16 toast points

Preheat the oven to 300 degrees. Melt the butter in a baking dish. Stir in the parsley, garlic, salt and pepper. Add the mushrooms and stir until well coated. Bake for 1 1/2 to 2 hours or until the mushrooms are a dark nutty brown, stirring occasionally. Serve on the toast points.

SERVES 4 TO 6

A Snail's Pace

Your guests may give you a quizzical look when you tell them the name of this dish is Champignon Escargots. There are no snails among the ingredients. Rather, the mushrooms, cooked slowly in garlic, butter, and parsley, simply mimic the famed French preparation of escargots. The secret to achieving the appropriate texture is slow-cooking at a relatively low temperature. The dish is best enjoyed if served to guests immediately after preparation.

Cheese and Pecan Stars

1 pound sharp Cheddar cheese,
   finely shredded
1½ cups all-purpose flour
¼ cup (½ stick) butter, softened

1 teaspoon salt
¼ teaspoon ground red pepper
½ cup chopped pecans

Preheat the oven to 375 degrees. Process the cheese, flour, butter, salt and red pepper in a food processor for 30 seconds or until the mixture forms a ball. Place the dough in a cookie press fitted with a star tip. Press onto an ungreased baking sheet. Top each star with a piece of pecan. Bake for 8 to 10 minutes or until light brown.

MAKES ABOUT 8 DOZEN

Baked Cheese Petits Fours

2 jars Old English sharp cheese
   spread, softened
1 cup (2 sticks) butter, softened
1 tablespoon Tabasco sauce
1 tablespoon Worcestershire sauce

2 tablespoons dill weed
½ teaspoon onion juice
½ teaspoon onion salt
2 loaves sliced white bread,
   crusts trimmed

Preheat the oven to 350 degrees. Beat the cheese spread and butter together in a mixing bowl until smooth. Add the Tabasco sauce, Worcestershire sauce, dill weed, onion juice and onion salt and beat until smooth. Spread a thin layer of cheese filling on 3 slices of the bread. Stack the slices on top of each other. Cut the stack into 4 quarters. Spread the cheese filling over the sides of each quarter. Repeat the procedure with the remaining filling and bread. Freeze the squares on a baking sheet for 1 hour. Bake for 15 to 20 minutes or until light brown. Serve hot.

SERVES 15

A New "Secret Recipe"

Baked Cheese Petits Fours are a new and savory twist on the traditionally sweet and fancifully iced version. Whether served as an appetizer or included on the table for a shower, tea, or coffee, these toasty cheese squares will have your guests asking for your "secret recipe." Preparation is made easy by freezing the squares before baking. For a larger gathering, double the recipe.

Grape Leaves

Stuffing
2 1/2 cups uncooked rice
4 teaspoons salt
1 1/2 teaspoons ground cinnamon
1 1/2 teaspoons black pepper
1/2 teaspoon red pepper

1 teaspoon ground allspice
1 (6-ounce) can tomato paste
2 1/2 pounds chili-ground chuck
1/2 cup (1 stick) butter, melted

Grape Leaves
1 (16-ounce) jar grape leaves,
   drained and rinsed, or 100 fresh
   grape leaves, rinsed

Assembly
Extra grape leaves or lemon slices
Salt and red pepper to taste
2 tablespoons butter
Lemon juice

For the stuffing, combine the rice, salt, cinnamon, black pepper, red pepper and allspice in a bowl and mix well. Stir in the tomato paste. Add the ground chuck and melted butter, using the hands to mix well. Microwave 1 teaspoon of the stuffing and 1 teaspoon water on high for 45 seconds or until done and taste for seasoning. Adjust the seasonings as necessary.

For the grape leaves, bring 3 inches of water to a boil in a large saucepan. Stack a few leaves at a time on a spatula and immerse in the boiling water. Blanch the jar leaves for 4 seconds or the fresh leaves for 2 seconds. Drain and remove to a baking sheet. Cut the stems from the base of the leaves and discard. Place each leaf smooth side down on a cutting board.

To assemble, place a heaping tablespoon of the stuffing on the leaf near the stem end; spread the stuffing across the leaf to form a small roll, leaving 1/2 inch on each side. Roll the stem end of the leaf over the stuffing. Tuck in the sides of the leaf and continue rolling to form a cigar shape.

To cook, line a large skillet with extra grape leaves or lemon slices. (A layer of beef or lamb bones, chicken wings or drumettes or beef cubes may be used.) Place the rolls in the pan close together in rows, alternating the direction of each row. Sprinkle with salt and red pepper. Dot with pats of the butter. Add a mixture of 1 part lemon juice and 2 parts water to barely cover the leaves. Place an inverted plate over the leaves to hold them in place. Bring to a boil. Reduce the heat to medium-low. Cook, covered, for 20 minutes. Reduce the heat to low. Cook for 30 minutes longer or until the rice is done and the leaves are tender.

MAKES 100

Prepared at Home

Whether served as an hors d'oeuvre during the cocktail hour, included with dinner as a side dish, or nestled alongside a green salad at lunch, grape leaves are at home on the South Louisiana table. While many hostesses rely on favorite Lebanese or Greek restaurants for their grape leaves, they may also prepare the dish at home with a bit of patience. Serve the prepared leaves either warm or chilled and accompanied by lemon wedges.

Spinach and Artichoke Pinwheels

1 (17-ounce) package frozen puff
    pastry sheets
1 (10-ounce) package frozen chopped
    spinach, thawed and squeezed dry
1 (14-ounce) can artichoke hearts,
    drained and finely chopped

1/2 cup (2 ounces) grated Parmesan cheese
1/4 cup mayonnaise
1 teaspoon garlic powder
1 teaspoon onion powder
1/2 teaspoon white pepper
1/2 teaspoon Cajun or Creole seasoning

Preheat the oven to 400 degrees. Thaw the puff pastry sheets for 30 minutes or until room temperature. Combine the spinach, artichoke hearts, cheese, mayonnaise, garlic powder, onion powder, white pepper and Cajun seasoning in a bowl and mix well. Unfold the pastry sheets on a lightly floured surface. Spread the spinach mixture evenly over both sheets, leaving a 1/2-inch border. Roll as for a jelly roll, sealing the seam. Wrap the rolls in heavy-duty plastic wrap. Freeze for 30 minutes. Cut into 1/2-inch slices. Place 1/2 inch apart on greased baking sheets. Bake for 10 to 12 minutes or until golden brown. Cool on a wire rack.

MAKES ABOUT 24

Spinach Cheese Squares

3 cups (12 ounces) shredded Monterey
    Jack cheese
2 1/2 cups (10 ounces) shredded sharp
    Cheddar cheese

2 (10-ounce) packages frozen chopped
    spinach, thawed and squeezed dry
6 eggs
Cajun or Creole seasoning to taste

Preheat the oven to 350 degrees. Combine the Monterey Jack cheese and Cheddar cheese in a bowl. Stir in the spinach. Add the eggs and Cajun seasoning and mix well. Pour into a greased 9×13-inch baking pan. Bake for 40 minutes. Let cool. Cut into desired-size servings.

SERVES 8

Two-Tomato Tapas

3 Roma tomatoes, chopped
12 sun-dried tomato halves, drained
  and chopped
1 cup (4 ounces) shredded Italian
  six-blend cheese
1/3 cup crumbled Gorgonzola or
  blue cheese

1/4 cup minced sweet onion
1 tablespoon chopped fresh basil
1 teaspoon chopped fresh rosemary
1/4 teaspoon garlic salt
1 baguette, cut into 1/4-inch slices

Preheat the oven to 350 degrees. Combine the Roma tomatoes, sun-dried tomatoes, Italian six-blend cheese, Gorgonzola cheese, onion, basil, rosemary and garlic salt in a bowl and mix well. Spoon onto the baguette slices. Bake for 7 to 8 minutes or until the cheese is melted.

MAKES 24 TAPAS

Half Time Buffalo Wings

Wings
1 (5-pound) bag chicken drumettes
  and elbows
2 teaspoons salt

1 teaspoon pepper
1 teaspoon garlic powder
1 teaspoon Cajun or Creole seasoning

Sauce
1/2 cup (1 stick) butter
1 cup hot red pepper sauce
2 tablespoons honey

1 tablespoon apple cider vinegar
1/2 tablespoon cayenne pepper

For the wings, arrange a single layer of the chicken pieces in a microwave-safe dish. Season with the salt, pepper, garlic powder and Cajun seasoning. Microwave on High for 30 minutes. Remove to a large bowl. Microwave the remaining chicken pieces in batches. Add the pieces to the bowl. Preheat the grill or broiler. Place the chicken pieces on a grill rack or in a large baking pan and grill over hot coals or broil until crisp.

For the sauce, melt the butter in a medium saucepan. Stir in the hot red pepper sauce, honey, vinegar and cayenne pepper. Simmer over low heat, stirring occasionally. (The longer the sauce simmers, the hotter it will be.) Pour over the crisp chicken pieces. Serve immediately.

SERVES 6

Oriental Chicken Wings

1/4 cup soy sauce
2 tablespoons vegetable oil
2 tablespoons chili sauce
1/4 cup honey
1 teaspoon salt

1/2 teaspoon ground ginger
1/4 teaspoon garlic powder
1/4 teaspoon cayenne pepper
3 pounds chicken wings,
    washed and dried

Combine the soy sauce, oil, chili sauce, honey, salt, ginger, garlic powder and cayenne pepper in a shallow dish. Add the chicken wings. Marinate in the refrigerator for 6 hours, turning occasionally. Preheat the oven to 375 degrees. Drain the chicken, reserving the marinade. Bake the chicken wings in a foil-lined broiler pan for 30 minutes. Baste with the reserved marinade. Bake for 30 minutes longer or until tender.

SERVES 10

Venison Hors d'Oeuvre

1 small bottle Italian salad dressing
2 tablespoons Worcestershire sauce
Garlic powder to taste
1 venison backstrap, sliced into
    thin medallions

8 ounces cream cheese, softened
1 jar jalapeño chile slices
1 pound sliced bacon
Salt and pepper to taste

Combine the Italian salad dressing, Worcestershire sauce and garlic powder in a shallow bowl. Add the venison medallions. Marinate in the refrigerator for 8 to 10 hours. Preheat the grill. Spread a thin layer of cream cheese over each venison medallion. Top with a jalapeño chile slice. Roll up each medallion tightly. Wrap each with a 2-inch piece of bacon and secure with a wooden pick. Place on a grill rack. Grill over hot coals for about 10 minutes. (Do not overcook.) Season lightly with salt and pepper.

SERVES 8

Shrimp Relish

1¹/2 pounds large shrimp, cooked,
   peeled and deveined
1 cup minced onion
1 cup snipped fresh parsley
2/3 cup vegetable oil

1/3 cup vinegar
1 garlic clove, minced
1¹/2 teaspoons salt
Dash of pepper

Combine the shrimp, onion and parsley in a large bowl. Beat the oil, vinegar, garlic, salt and pepper together in a small bowl. Pour over the shrimp. Marinate in the refrigerator for 1 hour or until serving time. Heap the shrimp in a serving bowl with a few arranged on the rim of the dish and serve with wooden picks as an appetizer. Or serve the shrimp on a bed of greens as a salad.

SERVES ABOUT 6 TO 8

English Cucumber Sandwiches

8 ounces cream cheese, softened
1 envelope Italian salad dressing mix
18 slices oatmeal bread (1 loaf)

1 English cucumber, sliced on an angle
Fresh or dried dill weed

Combine the cream cheese and salad dressing mix in a small bowl and mix well. Spread a thin layer of the cream cheese mixture over 9 slices of the oatmeal bread. Top each slice with 4 cucumber slices. Sprinkle with the dill weed and top with the remaining bread slices. Trim the crusts and cut each sandwich into 4 triangles.

Variation: For open-faced sandwiches, spread slices of the bread with the cream cheese mixture. Cut rounds from each bread slice using a 1¹/4- to 1¹/2-inch cutter (about 3 per slice). Top each round with a cucumber slice and dill weed.

MAKES 3 DOZEN

Roasted Chicken Salad Sandwiches

1 oven-roasted chicken, seasoned to
　taste, skinned, deboned and
　finely chopped
1 to 2 Red Delicious apples, peeled and
　puréed in a food processor
4 boiled eggs, finely chopped
1 teaspoon celery seeds
1 tablespoon prepared mustard

3/4 cup (or more) mayonnaise
1/2 cup sliced almonds, toasted
1/2 teaspoon white pepper
Cajun or Creole seasoning to taste
Butter, softened
18 slices white or wheat bread
　(1 loaf)

Combine the chicken, apples, eggs, celery seeds and mustard in a large bowl. Add enough of the mayonnaise to reach a desired consistency. Stir in the almonds, white pepper and Cajun seasoning. Butter the bread slices and spread 9 slices with the chicken mixture. Top with the remaining bread slices. Trim the crusts and cut each sandwich into 4 triangles.

MAKES 3 DOZEN

Carnival Crab Meat Dip

1/2 cup (1 stick) butter
3 green onions, chopped
1 teaspoon minced garlic
Dash of Tabasco sauce

12 ounces cream cheese, softened
1 pound lump crab meat, shells
　removed and flaked

Melt the butter in a medium saucepan over low heat. Add the green onions, garlic and Tabasco sauce and mix well. Stir in the cream cheese. Fold in the crab meat gently. Cook over low heat for 3 to 5 minutes or just until heated through. (Do not overcook.) Serve the dip warm with melba toast rounds or spoon into small puff pastry shells.

SERVES 12

Cold Shrimp Dip

1 cup sour cream
8 ounces cream cheese, softened
1 cup mayonnaise
2 tablespoons Worcestershire sauce
2 garlic cloves, minced

2 pounds shrimp, cooked, peeled
  and chopped
1 bunch green onions, chopped
Salt and pepper to taste
Tabasco sauce to taste

Combine the sour cream, cream cheese, mayonnaise, Worcestershire sauce and garlic in a bowl and mix well. Fold in the shrimp and green onions. Season with salt, pepper and Tabasco sauce to taste. Chill, covered, for 8 to 10 hours. Serve with crackers or chips.

SERVES 12

Crawfish Dip

1 cup finely chopped bell peppers
  (use a mixture of colors) (optional)
1 large onion, finely chopped
1/4 cup (1/2 stick) butter
1 pound fresh crawfish tails, peeled
2 or 3 garlic cloves, chopped

Red pepper to taste
Beau Monde seasoning or celery salt
  to taste
Cajun or Creole seasoning to taste
8 ounces cream cheese, cubed
Salt to taste

Sauté the bell peppers and onion in the butter in a large skillet until barely tender. Stir in the crawfish tails and garlic. Season with red pepper, Beau Monde seasoning and Cajun seasoning to taste. Cook for 10 to 15 minutes. Remove from the heat. Add the cream cheese and stir until melted. Add salt to taste. Chill for 2 hours before serving. Serve with crackers.

Note: You may use frozen crawfish tails, thawed and drained.

SERVES 6 TO 8

After the Season

When crawfish season comes to an end, South Louisiana cooks must make the occasional substitution in some of their favorite crawfish dishes. A substitution may also be necessary for those outside the region who have difficulty finding Louisiana crawfish tails at their market. Shrimp works equally well in most of these recipes. With this substitution, you can have your "crawfish" dip year-round.

Layered Seafood Dip

1 pound crawfish tails or shrimp
1/2 onion, finely chopped
1/4 cup (1/2 stick) butter
16 ounces cream cheese, softened
Tabasco sauce to taste
Worcestershire sauce to taste
Minced garlic to taste

Cajun or Creole seasoning to taste
1 bottle cocktail sauce, or 1 jar salsa
1 1/2 cups (6 ounces) shredded
  mozzarella cheese
1/2 green bell pepper, chopped
3 to 4 green onions chopped

Sauté the crawfish tails and onion in the butter in a large skillet until the onion is tender. Let cool. Combine the cream cheese with Tabasco sauce, Worcestershire sauce, garlic and Cajun seasoning to taste in a small bowl and mix well. Spread the cream cheese mixture on the bottom of a serving platter. Layer the crawfish mixture, cocktail sauce and mozzarella cheese over the cream cheese mixture. Sprinkle with the bell pepper and green onions. Chill until serving time. Serve with crackers.

SERVES 10 TO 12

Bacon, Lettuce and Tomato Dip

8 ounces cream cheese, softened
1 1/2 cups (about) mayonnaise
3/4 teaspoon salt
Pepper to taste
2 to 3 tomatoes, seeded and chopped

1 pound bacon, crisp-cooked and
  crumbled
1/2 large head lettuce, chopped into
  bite-size pieces

Mix the cream cheese with enough mayonnaise to reach salad dressing consistency in a large bowl. Add the salt and pepper. Stir in the tomatoes, bacon and lettuce. Serve with butter crackers.

SERVES 15

Baba Ghanoush

2 (1-pound) eggplant
3 tablespoons sesame tahini
2 tablespoons olive oil
3 tablespoons lemon juice
1/2 teaspoon salt

1/8 teaspoon red pepper
1/4 teaspoon garlic powder
Paprika to taste
Olive oil

Preheat the oven to 400 degrees. Pierce the eggplant several times with a fork. Bake on a baking sheet for 1 hour. Let cool. Cut lengthwise and scoop out the cooked eggplant, discarding as many seeds as possible. Combine the eggplant, sesame tahini, 2 tablespoons olive oil, lemon juice, salt, red pepper and garlic powder in a food processor and process for 5 seconds. Taste the mixture and adjust the seasonings if necessary. Add more lemon juice for a tangier taste. Process until smooth but not runny. Remove to a serving bowl. Chill, covered, until serving time. Sprinkle with paprika and cover with a thin layer of olive oil. Garnish with parsley sprigs or fresh mint. Serve with carrots, celery, toasted corn chips or toasted garlic pita chips.

SERVES 12 TO 15

Feta Cheese Spread

1 pound feta cheese, crumbled
3 ounces sun-dried tomatoes, chopped
1/4 cup chopped fresh parsley
4 garlic cloves, minced
2 tablespoons chopped fresh oregano, or
    2 teaspoons dried oregano

2 tablespoons chopped fresh thyme,
    or 2 teaspoons dried thyme
1 tablespoon red pepper flakes
1 cup (or more) olive oil

Combine the feta cheese, sun-dried tomatoes, parsley, garlic, oregano, thyme and red pepper flakes in a serving bowl and mix well. Pour the olive oil over the cheese mixture. (Do not stir.) Chill, covered with plastic wrap, for several hours. Stir well before serving. Serve with stone-ground wheat crackers or water crackers.

SERVES 10 TO 12

Hummus bi Tahini

1 (29-ounce) can chick-peas, drained,
   or 2 (14-ounce) cans chick-peas,
   drained
5 tablespoons sesame tahini
1/3 cup olive oil
1/3 cup lemon juice
1/3 cup cold water

1 teaspoon salt
1/2 teaspoon garlic powder, or
   minced garlic
1/4 teaspoon red pepper
Paprika to taste
Olive oil

Combine the chick-peas, sesame tahini, 1/3 cup olive oil, lemon juice, water, salt, garlic powder and red pepper in a food processor. (Be sure that the top layer of oil is mixed into the sesame tahini before measuring it.) Process until smooth. Taste and add more salt and red pepper if necessary. Add more lemon juice, olive oil or water to achieve desired taste and dip consistency. Remove to a serving bowl. Chill, covered, for several hours. Sprinkle with paprika. Pour a thin layer of olive oil over the top. Garnish with fresh mint, parsley, radishes, red bell peppers and/or olives.

SERVES 10 TO 12

A Versatile Snack

Everyone knows that hummus is a healthful dip, one often enjoyed with pita bread wedges or corn chips. However, hummus also makes a tasty vegetarian sandwich when spread inside a pita pocket and layered with crisp vegetables and a spoonful or two of tabouli. Hummus is practical as well as versatile, as it can be refrigerated for five to seven days. Keep it on hand for an after-school snack or an impromptu appetizer.

Pesto Feta Cheese Loaf

1 cup (2 sticks) unsalted butter,
  cut into pieces
12 ounces feta cheese, crumbled
8 ounces cream cheese, softened
2 garlic cloves, minced
1 green onion, minced
3 tablespoons dry vermouth

1/2 teaspoon white pepper
6 drops of Tabasco sauce
1 (8-ounce) package sun-dried
  tomatoes
1 cup pesto
1/2 cup pine nuts, toasted

Combine the butter, feta cheese, cream cheese, garlic, green onion and vermouth in a food processor. Process until smooth. Add the pepper and Tabasco sauce and process until well combined. Soak the sun-dried tomatoes in hot water for 30 minutes; drain well and chop finely. Drain some of the olive oil from the pesto to prevent the loaf from becoming runny.

To assemble, line a loaf pan with long strips of plastic wrap, leaving a wide margin of wrap overlapping the pan. Layer all of the pine nuts, 1/3 of the tomatoes, 1/3 of the pesto and 1/3 of the cheese mixture in the pan. Repeat the layers 2 more times with the remaining tomatoes, pesto and cheese mixture. Fold the plastic wrap over the pan and press the layers down. Store in the freezer. Place the pan in the refrigerator to defrost about 24 hours before serving. Invert onto a serving platter. Garnish with fresh basil, tomatoes or fruit. Serve with plain crackers.

SERVES 30

Mexican Dip

16 ounces cream cheese, softened
2 (15-ounce) cans black beans, drained
1 (10-ounce) can tomatoes with
  green chiles

2 cups (8 ounces) shredded Mexican-
  blend cheese

Preheat the oven to 350 degrees. Mash the cream cheese in the bottom of a pie plate and spread to form an even layer. Layer the black beans, tomatoes with green chiles and Mexican-blend cheese over the cream cheese. Bake for 15 minutes or until the cheese is melted. Serve warm with corn chips.

SERVES 10 TO 12

Onion Soufflé

3 ounces cream cheese, softened
1 cup (4 ounces) freshly grated
    Parmesan cheese

1 1/2 cups frozen chopped onions,
    thawed
1/4 cup mayonnaise

Preheat the oven to 400 degrees. Combine the cream cheese, Parmesan cheese, onions and mayonnaise in a bowl and mix well. Spoon into a greased 1-quart soufflé dish. Bake for 20 minutes or until brown on top. Store leftover soufflé in the refrigerator and reheat as needed.

SERVES 10 TO 12

Pepper Jelly Cheese Dip

2 cups (8 ounces) shredded
    Cheddar cheese
1/4 cup light mayonnaise
Cajun or Creole seasoning to taste

1/2 cup red or green jalapeño chile jelly
1/2 cup pecans, toasted and ground
1/2 cup finely chopped green onion tops

Combine the cheese, mayonnaise and Cajun seasoning in a bowl and mix well. Spread in the bottom of a pie plate or shallow serving dish. Spread the jalapeño chile jelly over the cheese layer. Top with the pecans and green onions. Serve with wheat crackers, pita chips or bagel chips.

SERVES 12

Black Bean Salsa

3 small avocados, diced
1 red bell pepper, diced
1 (11-ounce) can white Shoe Peg
   corn, drained
1 (15-ounce) can black beans, drained
   and rinsed

1 bunch cilantro, finely chopped
   (leaves only)
1 bunch green onions, chopped
   (tops and half of bottoms)
3/4 cup Italian salad dressing
   with olive oil

Combine the avocados, bell pepper, corn, black beans, cilantro, green onions and Italian dressing in a bowl and mix well. Chill until serving time. Serve with tostada scoops or corn chips.

SERVES 8 TO 10

Cilantro Salsa

1 (10-ounce) can tomatoes with
   green chiles
1 (4-ounce) can green chiles
1 (4-ounce) can chopped black olives
1 cup (4 ounces) shredded Monterey
   Jack cheese

1/4 cup Italian salad dressing
4 green onions, finely chopped
   (snip with scissors)
1/4 cup chopped fresh cilantro
   (snip with scissors)

Combine the tomatoes, green chiles, olives, cheese, salad dressing, green onions and cilantro in a bowl and mix well. Chill for 8 to 10 hours. Serve with tortilla chips.

SERVES 10 TO 15

Cheesy Spinach Dip

1 (1¹/2-pound) round loaf
    sourdough bread
¹/3 cup butter
²/3 cup chopped red bell pepper

¹/3 cup chopped onion
1 pound Velveeta cheese, cubed
1 (10-ounce) package frozen chopped
    spinach, cooked and drained

Preheat the oven to 350 degrees. Cut a horizontal slice from the top of the bread. Remove the soft bread center from the loaf, leaving a 1-inch shell. Cut the removed bread into bite-size cubes. Brush the inside of the shell with 3 tablespoons of the butter. Place the shell and the bread cubes on a baking sheet. Bake for 20 minutes or until crisp and brown. Sauté the bell pepper and onion in the remaining butter in a skillet until tender. Add the cheese and cook until melted, stirring constantly. Stir in the spinach. Cook until heated through, stirring constantly. Pour into the bread shell. Serve the dip with the bread cubes and assorted fresh vegetables.

MAKES 2²/3 CUPS

Hot Mexican Spinach Dip

1 (16-ounce) jar hot salsa
1 (10-ounce) package frozen chopped
    spinach, thawed and squeezed dry
8 ounces cream cheese, diced and
    softened

2 cups (8 ounces) shredded
    Monterey Jack cheese
1 cup evaporated milk
1 tablespoon red wine vinegar

Preheat the oven to 400 degrees. Combine the salsa, spinach, cream cheese, Monterey Jack cheese, evaporated milk and vinegar in a baking dish and mix well. Bake for 15 to 20 minutes or until bubbly. Serve with freshly toasted baguette slices or tortilla chips.

SERVES 10

Fruit and Yogurt Dip

8 ounces cream cheese, softened
2 cups strawberry-orange yogurt
2 tablespoons brown sugar
1 teaspoon lemon juice
1 (8-ounce) can crushed pineapple,
   drained

3/4 cup flaked coconut
Grated orange zest
Assorted fresh fruits for dipping,
   such as strawberries, cantaloupe,
   kiwifruit, apples and oranges

Beat the cream cheese at medium speed in a mixing bowl until fluffy. Add the yogurt, brown sugar and lemon juice and beat until smooth. Stir in the pineapple and coconut. Spoon the dip into a serving bowl and sprinkle with grated orange zest. Serve with assorted fruits.

SERVES 25 TO 30

Cranberry Jalapeño Relish

2 cups fresh cranberries
1/4 cup diced red onion
1 large jalapeño chile, seeded and diced

2 tablespoons lime juice
1/2 teaspoon ground ginger
1/2 cup sugar

Coarsely chop the cranberries in a food processor. Bring the cranberries to a boil in a saucepan. Simmer for 1 or 2 minutes, stirring constantly. Combine the cranberries, onion, jalapeño chile, lime juice, ginger and sugar in a bowl and mix well. Chill for 24 hours before serving. Serve as a side to poultry or spoon over a block of cream cheese and serve with crackers.

SERVES 15

Appletini

1 ounce sour apple liqueur
1 ounce lemon vodka
Ice

Shake the sour apple liqueur and vodka with ice in a martini shaker. Pour into a martini glass. Garnish with apple slices dipped in lemon.

SERVES 1

Bellinis

6 cups sliced fresh peaches, or frozen
peaches, thawed

2 cups apricot nectar
6 to 7 cups Champagne

Combine 1/2 of the peaches and 1/2 of the apricot nectar in a blender and process until smooth. Repeat with the remaining peaches and apricot nectar. Freeze the purée in a freezer container. Remove from the freezer 1 hour before serving. Spoon about 2/3 cup of the purée into each stemmed glass. Add 2/3 cup of the Champagne.

SERVES 10

A Springtime Libation

Although originating along the canals of Venice, Italy, the Bellini is a welcome addition to the tables of South Louisiana. The refreshing apricot and peach flavors make this drink popular at warm-weather gatherings. For a bit of Italian authenticity, consider using white peaches, if available, and Prosecco, a dry Italian sparkling wine. If, like us, you use Champagne, buy Brut or Extra Brut, the two driest Champagne types.

Cajun Bloody Marys

1 quart beefamato juice
1 quart clamato juice
5 tablespoons Worcestershire sauce
3 tablespoons lime juice

1 tablespoon Tabasco sauce
2 cups vodka
Cajun or Creole seasoning to taste
Lime halves

Combine the beefamato juice, clamato juice, Worcestershire sauce, lime juice, Tabasco sauce, vodka and Cajun seasoning in a large pitcher and stir well. Chill for 24 hours for the best flavor. Rub cut lime halves around the rim of the pitcher, scraping a little pulp into the mixture. Serve over ice.

SERVES 10

Christmas Cosmopolitan

2 ounces vodka
1/2 ounce Triple Sec
1/2 ounce cranberry juice

1/2 ounce lime juice
Ice

Shake the vodka, Triple Sec, cranberry juice and lime juice with ice in a shaker. Strain into a martini glass. Garnish with a wedge of lime.

SERVES 1

Kir Royale

8 teaspoons crème de cassis
1 bottle of chilled Champagne
4 lemon twists

Pour 2 teaspoons of the crème de cassis in each of 4 tall Champagne flutes. Fill each glass with Champagne and garnish each with a lemon twist. Serve immediately.

SERVES 4

Red Rooster

3 cups orange juice
3 cups cranberry juice
3 cups vodka

Combine the orange juice, cranberry juice and vodka in a large shallow freezer container. Freeze for 24 hours or until slushy. Serve as a slush.

SERVES 10

Namesake Punch

Each Provisional Class of the Junior League of Lafayette is treated to a Red Rooster Party. Held in a member's home and hosted by the previous year's Provisional Class, the Red Rooster Party allows the new members to get to know their fellow members in a casual, relaxed environment. The party's namesake punch adds to the festivities. Red Rooster is beautiful when served in a crystal bowl or pitcher.

Iced Cappuccino

1¹/2 cups strong coffee
¹/2 cup sweetened condensed milk

¹/2 cup half-and-half
1 teaspoon vanilla extract

Combine the coffee and condensed milk in a 2-quart pitcher. Whisk in the half-and-half and vanilla. Pour into ice-filled glasses. Serve with dark chocolate cookies or shortbread cookies.

SERVES 6 TO 8

Whiskey Slush

1 liter lemon-lime soda
1 cup sugar
8 ounces frozen strawberries, puréed
1 (20-ounce) can crushed pineapple
    with juice
2¹/2 cups pineapple juice

1 (6-ounce) can frozen limeade
    concentrate
1 (6-ounce) can frozen fruit punch
    concentrate
1 cup orange juice
1 cup whiskey

Combine the lemon-lime soda, sugar, strawberry purée, pineapple, pineapple juice, limeade concentrate, fruit punch concentrate, orange juice and whiskey in a large shallow freezer container. Freeze for 24 hours or until slushy, stirring frequently. Serve as a slush.

SERVES 10

Equally Suited

Slightly sinful, yet beautifully pink, Whiskey Slush is as suited for the men at the Camp as it is for the ladies' afternoon card game. The frosty punch is delicious for either occasion and can be ladled from a punch bowl or, if thawed a bit more, poured from a pitcher. Stir the punch frequently as it freezes to ensure that it remains slushy. Allow adequate time to thaw to the desired consistency before serving.

Pitcher Perfect Lemonade

1 dozen lemons, juiced (small, thin-
  skinned lemons have more juice)
3/4 gallon water, at room temperature

4 cups sugar
Ice
Vodka (optional)

Pour the lemon juice into a 1-gallon jar. Stir in the water. Add the sugar and stir until dissolved. Fill the jar to the top with ice. Add vodka as desired to make an adult beverage.

SERVES 10 TO 15

Jester's Milk Punch

3 cups vanilla ice cream
1 cup milk
1/2 cup bourbon

1/4 cup white crème de cacao, or light rum
3 tablespoons brandy
Freshly grated nutmeg

Combine the ice cream, milk, bourbon, crème de cacao and brandy in a blender and blend until smooth. Pour into chilled Champagne glasses or punch cups. Sprinkle nutmeg over the top.

SERVES 5 TO 6

Southern Belle Punch

3 1/4 cups sugar
6 cups water
1 (46-ounce) can pineapple juice
1 (12-ounce) can frozen orange juice
   concentrate

1 (6-ounce) can frozen lemonade
   concentrate
5 ripe bananas
1 liter ginger ale

Combine the sugar and water in a large saucepan. Bring to a boil and stir until the sugar is dissolved. Remove from the heat. Stir in the pineapple juice, orange juice concentrate and lemonade concentrate. Combine the bananas and a little of the juice mixture in a food processor and process until smooth. Add the banana purée to the juice mixture and mix well. Freeze a portion of the mixture in a bundt pan or other decorative pan.

To serve, unmold the frozen mixture into a punch bowl. Add 4 to 5 cups of the unfrozen mixture to the bowl. Stir in the ginger ale.

SERVES 20

Spiced Tea

2 cups Tang
1 cup sugar
1 small envelope sugar-free lemonade
   drink mix

1 cup instant tea
1/2 teaspoon ground cloves
1/2 teaspoon ground cinnamon

Combine the Tang, sugar, lemonade drink mix, instant tea, cloves and cinnamon in a jar and shake well. Add the mix 1 teaspoon at a time to a mug of hot water until desired taste is reached.

MAKES ABOUT 4 CUPS MIX, ENOUGH FOR ABOUT 50 TO 60 SERVINGS

Cinnamon Pecans

While sipping on Spiced Tea, your afternoon guests will enjoy nibbling on a few Cinnamon Pecans. Melt 1/4 cup (1/2 stick) butter in a microwave-safe dish. Stir in 1/2 cup sugar, 2 tablespoons water, 1 teaspoon ground cinnamon and 1/4 teaspoon salt. Add 4 cups pecan halves, stirring to coat well. Microwave for 10 minutes, stirring every 2 to 3 minutes. Pour the pecans onto waxed paper and separate the pecans. (The pecans will harden as they cool.) Makes 4 cups.

Breads & Breakfast

Crawfish Corn Bread

2 cups white cornmeal
2 tablespoons sugar
1 teaspoon baking soda
2 teaspoons salt
3 eggs
1 onion, minced

2 cups (8 ounces) shredded
   Cheddar cheese
1/3 cup vegetable oil
1 (15-ounce) can cream-style corn
1 pound crawfish tails, chopped

Preheat the oven to 375 degrees. Combine the cornmeal, sugar, baking soda and salt in a bowl. Beat the eggs in another bowl and stir in the onion, cheese, oil and corn. Pour into the cornmeal mixture and mix well. Pour the batter into a 9×12-inch baking dish coated with nonstick cooking spray. Sprinkle the chopped crawfish tails evenly over the batter. Bake for 45 minutes or until golden brown.

SERVES 12

Jalapeño Hush Puppies

2 cups cornmeal
1 cup all-purpose flour
2 tablespoons baking powder
1/4 cup minced onion
1/4 cup finely chopped seeded
   jalapeño chiles

1 egg
2 tablespoons vegetable oil or
   bacon drippings
Cajun or Creole seasoning to taste
Milk
Vegetable oil for frying

Combine the cornmeal, flour, baking powder, onion, jalapeño chiles, egg, oil and Cajun seasoning in a large bowl and mix well. Add just enough milk to form a thick batter. Shape into 1/2-inch balls, using buttered hands. Drop into 375-degree oil. Fry until golden brown. Drain on paper towels.

MAKES 2 DOZEN

Parker House Rolls

2 envelopes dry yeast
1 teaspoon sugar
1/4 cup lukewarm water
3 rounded tablespoons shortening
　(about 1/3 cup)
2 cups milk

2 teaspoons salt
1/2 cup sugar
1 egg, beaten
6 to 7 cups unsifted all-purpose flour
Melted butter

Dissolve the yeast and 1 teaspoon sugar in the water. Heat the shortening in 1 cup of the milk in a small saucepan, stirring until the shortening is melted. Cool to lukewarm. Stir in the remaining 1 cup milk, salt, 1/2 cup sugar, egg and yeast mixture. Stir in the flour 2 cups at a time, adding enough of the flour to make a soft dough (The dough should not be sticky.) Knead on a floured surface until smooth and elastic. Place in a greased bowl, turning to coat the surface. Let rise, covered, in a warm place for 1 1/2 hours or until doubled in bulk.

Punch the dough down and knead until smooth. Divide the dough into halves. Roll into 1/2-inch-thick circles on a lightly floured surface. Cut with a biscuit cutter. Brush each round with melted butter. Make an indentation across each round with a knife. Fold over and pinch edges together. Place on a greased baking sheet. Brush the tops with melted butter. (The rolls may be frozen on a baking sheet, then wrapped and stored in the freezer. The frozen rolls will need to rise for 4 to 5 hours to double in bulk.) Let rise for 1 1/2 to 2 hours or until doubled in bulk. Preheat the oven to 400 degrees. Bake for 10 to 12 minutes or until golden brown.

MAKES 3 DOZEN

California Artichoke Bread

1 (1-pound) loaf French bread
6 garlic cloves, chopped
1/2 cup (1 stick) butter
1 1/2 cups sour cream
1 (14-ounce) can artichoke hearts,
    drained
1 (6-ounce) can sliced black olives

8 ounces Monterey Jack cheese with
    pepper, cubed
1/4 cup (1 ounce) grated
    Parmesan cheese
2 tablespoons chopped fresh parsley
1 tablespoon lemon pepper

Preheat the oven to 350 degrees. Cut the French bread into halves lengthwise. Remove the soft bread from the shells in small chunks. Sauté the garlic briefly in the butter in a large skillet. Add the bread chunks and sauté until golden. Remove from the heat. Add the sour cream, artichoke hearts, black olives, Monterey Jack cheese, Parmesan cheese, parsley and lemon pepper and mix well. Spoon into both of the bread shells. Bake each half separately for 20 to 30 minutes.

SERVES 6 TO 8

Poppy Seed Puff Pastry Straws

1 (17-ounce) package frozen puff
    pastry, thawed
1 egg, beaten
1 tablespoon water

1/4 cup (1 ounce) grated
    Parmesan cheese
2 tablespoons poppy seeds
1 teaspoon dried parsley flakes

Preheat the oven to 375 degrees. Unfold the 2 pastry sheets on a lightly floured surface. Beat the egg and water together in a small bowl. Brush the egg mixture over the pastry sheets. Sprinkle with the cheese, poppy seeds and parsley flakes. Cut each sheet in half lengthwise. Cut crosswise into 26 (1/2-inch) strips. Place the strips 2 inches apart on a greased baking sheet. Bake for 10 to 12 minutes or until golden. Serve alone as an appetizer or along with a salad.

MAKES 52

Made in Minutes

No need to serve soups and salads alone or with the usual crackers. Poppy Seed Puff Pastry Straws are simple to make and will quickly spruce up your salad course. Place two or three straws alongside or on top of your salad. They are a natural accompaniment to Fruity Spring Mix Salad (page 123). If salad is not on your menu, serve a batch of straws as a tasty appetizer.

Italian Loaf

1 pound smoked sausage, thinly sliced
1 (1-pound) loaf frozen white bread,
    thawed
1/2 cup (1 stick) butter, melted
1 large jar sliced olives with pimento,
    drained (optional)

1 cup (4 ounces) grated
    Parmesan cheese
1/3 cup grated Romano cheese
2 teaspoons Cajun or Creole seasoning
1 egg, beaten

Preheat the oven to 350 degrees. Cook the sausage in boiling water to cover for 8 to 10 minutes; drain. Slice the bread dough into halves. Roll each half into a rectangle on a lightly floured surface. Brush with some of the melted butter. Arrange the sausage slices over the rectangles, leaving a 1/2-inch margin of dough. Sprinkle with the sliced olives, Parmesan cheese, Romano cheese and Cajun seasoning. Roll the dough to enclose the filling, tucking in the ends. Place the loaves seam side down on a baking sheet. Brush with the egg. Bake for 20 to 25 minutes or until golden brown. Let cool on a wire rack.

SERVES 6 TO 8

A Hearty Appetizer

When thinly sliced and served hot, Italian Loaf makes a hearty contribution to a holiday buffet or a cocktail-hour gathering. For convenience, the loaves can be fully prepared and then wrapped and frozen for several months. When needed, thaw the loaves fully and warm in a 325-degree oven. When heated through, slice and serve hot.

Spinach Cheese Loaf

1 pound Monterey Jack cheese with
  pepper, shredded
1 (10-ounce) package frozen spinach,
  thawed and squeezed dry
1 cup mayonnaise

4 sun-dried tomatoes, thinly sliced
1 teaspoon garlic salt
Butter, softened
1 (1-pound) loaf French bread,
  sliced into halves lengthwise

Preheat the oven to 350 degrees. Combine the cheese, spinach, mayonnaise, sun-dried tomatoes and garlic salt in a bowl and mix well. Spread a thin layer of butter on each bread half. Spread 1/2 of the cheese mixture over each bread half. Bake for 20 minutes or until the cheese is melted and bubbly.

MAKES 20 SERVINGS

Swiss Cheese Loaf

1 (1-pound) loaf French bread
1 cup (2 sticks) butter, melted
2 tablespoons grated onion
1 tablespoon yellow mustard

2 tablespoons lemon juice
1/2 teaspoon Beau Monde seasoning
8 ounces Swiss cheese slices

Preheat the oven to 350 degrees. Cut the bread into 11/2-inch slices, leaving the slices attached at the bottom of the loaf. Place the bread on a foil-lined baking sheet. Bring the foil up around the loaf to form a boat. Combine the butter, onion, yellow mustard, lemon juice and Beau Monde seasoning in a bowl and mix well. Place a cheese slice between each bread slice. Spread some of the butter mixture between the bread slices and over the top of the loaf. Bake for 30 minutes.

Note: The bread may be frozen before baking.

SERVES 8 TO 10

Royal Drop Biscuits

2 cups all-purpose flour
1 tablespoon baking powder
1/2 teaspoon salt

1/4 cup shortening
1 cup milk

Preheat the oven to 450 degrees. Combine the flour, baking powder and salt in a bowl. Cut in the shortening until crumbly. Add the milk and stir just until mixed. Drop by spoonfuls onto a greased baking sheet. Bake for 10 to 12 minutes or until golden brown.

SERVES 6 TO 8

Blueberry Crostata

1 1/4 cups all-purpose flour
3/4 cup granulated sugar
1/8 teaspoon salt
1/2 cup (1 stick) butter, softened
1 egg, lightly beaten
1 tablespoon all-purpose flour

2 tablespoons granulated sugar
2 cups fresh blueberries
1 tablespoon lemon juice
1 egg, lightly beaten
1 tablespoon turbinado sugar

Preheat the oven to 375 degrees. Combine 1 1/4 cups flour, 3/4 cup granulated sugar and salt in a large bowl. Add the butter and 1 egg, stirring to form a soft dough. Shape into a 4-inch round. Place the round on a flour-dusted sheet of parchment paper. Roll the dough into a 10-inch circle. Transfer the parchment paper and dough circle to a baking sheet. Chill, covered with plastic wrap, for 10 minutes. Combine 1 tablespoon flour and 2 tablespoons granulated sugar in a small bowl. Spread over the chilled dough round, leaving a 1-inch edge. Spoon the berries over the dough. Sprinkle with the lemon juice. Fold the 1-inch border of dough over the berries. Brush the egg over the dough edges. Sprinkle the turbinado sugar over the top. Bake for 35 minutes. Cool on a wire rack for 1 hour. Serve warm or at room temperature.

SERVES 6 TO 8

Turbinado Sugar

Blueberry Crostata is sprinkled with turbinado sugar prior to baking. What is turbinado sugar? This is a form of raw sugar that retains a touch of natural molasses flavor in the preparation of its coarse granules. The molasses is what gives turbinado its light brown color. If you can't find this product in your local supermarket, you'll find it on the shelves of your natural foods store.

Cream Cheese Danish Squares

2 (8-ounce) cans refrigerated
   crescent rolls
1 egg yolk
16 ounces cream cheese, softened
1 cup granulated sugar

1 teaspoon lemon juice
1 teaspoon vanilla extract
1 egg white, lightly beaten
3/4 cup chopped pecans
Confectioners' sugar

Preheat the oven to 375 degrees. Unroll the dough from 1 can of crescent rolls. Press into a lightly greased 9×13-inch baking pan. Beat the the egg yolk and the next 4 ingredients in a small bowl until smooth. Spread over the crescent roll layer. Unroll the dough from the remaining can of rolls. Press into a 9×13-inch rectangle on a sheet of waxed paper. Place the dough over the layer of cream cheese mixture. Brush with the egg white. Sprinkle with the pecans. Bake for 25 minutes. Sprinkle with confectioners' sugar. Let cool in the pan. Cut into squares.

SERVES 10

Mardi Gras Coffee Cake

1 1/2 cups all-purpose flour
3/4 cup granulated sugar
1 tablespoon baking powder
1/2 teaspoon salt
1/4 cup shortening
2 small eggs, beaten
1/2 cup milk

1 teaspoon vanilla extract
1/2 cup packed brown sugar
2 tablespoons all-purpose flour
2 teaspoons ground cinnamon
1/2 cup raisins (optional)
2 tablespoons butter, melted

Preheat the oven to 375 degrees. Combine the flour, granulated sugar, baking powder and salt in a bowl. Cut in the shortening until crumbly. Combine the eggs, milk and vanilla in a small bowl and mix well. Add to the flour mixture and stir just until blended. Combine the brown sugar, 2 tablespoons flour, cinnamon and raisins in a bowl and mix well. Stir in the melted butter. Spoon 2/3 of the batter into a greased and floured 9-inch cake pan. Sprinkle evenly with the brown sugar mixture. Top with the remaining batter. Bake for 20 minutes.

SERVES 6 TO 8

A Festive Topping

If serving Mardi Gras Coffee Cake during the Mardi Gras season, consider a glaze that mimics the traditional King Cake and looks beautiful on your buffet table. After preparing the coffee cake as directed, combine 1 cup sifted confectioners' sugar with 1 to 2 tablespoons lemon juice or water or just enough to reach a drizzling consistency. Drizzle the glaze over the cake and decorate with purple, green, and gold sugars or candies.

Easy Pumpkin Swirl

Cake

3 eggs
1 cup granulated sugar
2/3 cup canned pumpkin
3/4 cup buttermilk baking mix
2 teaspoons ground cinnamon

1 teaspoon pumpkin pie spice
1/2 teaspoon grated nutmeg
1 cup chopped nuts
Confectioners' sugar

Filling

1 cup confectioners' sugar
8 ounces cream cheese, softened

6 tablespoons butter, softened
1 teaspoon vanilla extract

For the cake, preheat the oven to 375 degrees. Combine the eggs and granulated sugar in a bowl and beat until fluffy. Stir in the pumpkin. Combine the baking mix, cinnamon, pumpkin pie spice and nutmeg in a bowl and mix well. Add to the egg mixture and stir just until mixed. Stir in the nuts. Pour into a 10×15-inch baking pan lined with waxed paper or parchment paper. Bake for 13 to 15 minutes or until the cake tests done. Dust a clean kitchen towel with confectioners' sugar. Invert the cake onto the towel. Remove the waxed paper. Roll the warm cake in the towel as for a jelly roll from the short side and place on a wire rack to cool.

For the filling, cream the confectioners' sugar, cream cheese, butter and vanilla in a bowl.

To assemble, unroll the cooled cake carefully and remove the towel. Spread the filling over the cake and reroll. Chill until serving time.

SERVES 8 TO 10

Banana Muffins

1 1/2 cups all-purpose flour
1 teaspoon baking powder
1 teaspoon baking soda
1/2 teaspoon salt
3 bananas, mashed
3/4 cup granulated sugar

1 egg, lightly beaten
1/3 cup butter, melted
1/3 cup packed brown sugar
2 tablespoons all-purpose flour
1/2 teaspoon ground cinnamon
1 tablespoon butter

Preheat the oven to 375 degrees. Combine 1 1/2 cups flour, baking powder, baking soda and salt in a large bowl. Beat the bananas, granulated sugar, egg and 1/3 cup butter together in a bowl. Add to the dry ingredients and stir just until mixed. Spoon into 12 greased or paper-lined muffin cups. Combine the brown sugar, 2 tablespoons flour and cinnamon in a small bowl. Cut in 1 tablespoon butter until crumbly. Sprinkle over the muffins. Bake for 18 to 20 minutes or until the tops are firm.

MAKES 1 DOZEN

Blueberry Muffins

3/4 cup (1 1/2 sticks) butter, softened
1 cup sugar
3/4 cup milk
1 egg
1 3/4 cups all-purpose flour

2 1/2 teaspoons baking powder
1/2 teaspoon salt
1 cup fresh blueberries
1 tablespoon all-purpose flour

Preheat the oven to 400 degrees. Cream the butter and sugar in a mixing bowl until light and fluffy. Beat in the milk and egg. Combine 1 3/4 cups flour, baking powder and salt in a bowl. Add to the creamed mixture and stir just until mixed. Toss the blueberries with 1 tablespoon flour. Fold the blueberries gently into the batter. Fill 12 greased or paper-lined muffin cups 2/3 full. Bake for 20 minutes or until the tops are firm.

MAKES 1 DOZEN

Spiced Pumpkin Muffins

2 cups all-purpose flour
2/3 cup packed brown sugar
1/3 cup granulated sugar
1 tablespoon baking powder
1/4 teaspoon baking soda
1 teaspoon salt
1 teaspoon ground cinnamon

1/4 teaspoon ground ginger
1/4 teaspoon ground nutmeg
1/2 cup (1 stick) butter, melted
1/2 cup canned pumpkin
1/3 cup milk
2 eggs, slightly beaten

Preheat the oven to 400 degrees. Combine the flour, brown sugar, granulated sugar, baking powder, baking soda, salt, cinnamon, ginger and nutmeg in a large bowl and mix well. Beat the butter, pumpkin, milk and eggs together in a bowl. Add to the dry ingredients and stir just until mixed. Spoon into 12 greased or paper-lined muffin cups. Bake for 15 to 20 minutes or until the tops are firm. Cool for 5 minutes. Remove from the pan.

MAKES 1 DOZEN

Cinnamon Bread Soufflé

10 cups cubed cinnamon bread
8 ounces cream cheese, softened
8 eggs
1 1/2 cups milk

2/3 cup half-and-half
1/2 cup maple syrup
1/2 teaspoon vanilla extract
2 tablespoons confectioners' sugar

Place the bread cubes in a lightly greased 9×13-inch baking pan. Beat the cream cheese in a mixing bowl until smooth. Beat in the eggs 1 at a time. Add the milk, half-and-half, maple syrup and vanilla and mix well. Pour over the bread cubes. Chill for 8 to 10 hours. Let stand at room temperature for 30 minutes before baking. Preheat the oven to 375 degrees. Bake, uncovered, for 30 minutes or until a knife inserted in the center comes out clean. Sprinkle with the confectioners' sugar. Serve warm with maple syrup.

SERVES 10 TO 12

Oven French Toast

1 loaf French bread, cut into 1 1/2- to
    2-inch slices
6 eggs, beaten
1 1/2 cups milk
1 1/2 cups half-and-half
2 teaspoons vanilla extract

1/4 teaspoon grated nutmeg
1/4 teaspoon ground cinnamon
1/2 cup (1 stick) margarine, softened
1 cup chopped nuts
1 cup packed brown sugar
2 tablespoons dark corn syrup

Arrange the bread slices in a greased 9×13-inch baking dish. Combine the eggs, milk, half-and-half, vanilla, nutmeg and cinnamon in a bowl and mix well. Pour over the bread. Chill for 12 to 14 hours. Preheat the oven to 350 degrees. Combine the margarine, nuts, brown sugar and corn syrup in a small bowl and mix well. Spoon evenly over the bread. Bake for 40 minutes.

SERVES 8 TO 10

Pain Perdu

Can't find what you are looking for? French toast may appear on a Louisiana menu as *pain perdu*, meaning "lost bread." The reason for the name is understandable—day-old bread is quickly reclaimed in this dish as it soaks up the recipe's rich ingredients. Although you will find this Oven French Toast is decadent on its own, offer a pitcher of warmed maple syrup at the table. You and your guests will find it hard to resist.

Artichoke Squares

2 (6-ounce) jars marinated
  artichoke hearts
1 small onion, finely chopped
1 garlic clove, minced
4 eggs

8 ounces Cheddar cheese, shredded
1/4 cup Italian-style bread crumbs
2 tablespoons minced fresh parsley
1/4 teaspoon salt
1/8 teaspoon dried oregano

Preheat the oven to 350 degrees. Drain the marinade from the artichoke hearts into a skillet. Chop the artichoke hearts. Sauté the onion and garlic in the artichoke marinade until the onion is translucent. Beat the eggs in a bowl until frothy. Add the cheese, bread crumbs, parsley, salt and oregano and mix well. Stir in the onion mixture and chopped artichokes. Pour into a greased 7×11-inch or 9×9-inch baking pan. Bake for 30 minutes. Cool in the pan. Cut into 1-inch squares. Reheat the squares for 10 minutes before serving, if desired.

SERVES 8

Spinach Portobello Quiche

1 (10-ounce) package frozen chopped
  spinach, thawed and squeezed dry
1/2 cup chopped portobello
  mushroom cap
1/4 onion, chopped
1 (4-ounce) can diced green chiles
1 teaspoon Cajun or Creole seasoning
Dash of Tabasco sauce
Salt and pepper to taste

1 unbaked (10-inch) deep-dish pie shell
1/4 cup (1 ounce) shredded cheese
  (Cheddar, feta, Monterey Jack with
  pepper or a mixture)
3 eggs, beaten, or use an equivalent
  amount of egg substitute
1/4 to 1/3 cup milk
2 tablespoons sour cream
Butter

Preheat the oven to 375 degrees. Combine the spinach, mushroom, onion, green chiles, Cajun seasoning, Tabasco sauce, salt and pepper in a bowl and mix well. Pour into the pie shell. Sprinkle the cheese over the top. Combine the eggs, milk and sour cream in a bowl and beat until frothy. Pour over the cheese. Dot with butter. Bake for 1 hour or until golden brown.

SERVES 6

Breakfast Corn Bread Casserole

2¹/2 pounds ground beef
Onion powder to taste
Garlic powder to taste
Salt and red pepper to taste
2 (6-ounce) packages corn bread mix
2 eggs

1/2 cup milk
1/2 cup diced jalapeño chiles
1 (15-ounce) can cream-style corn
24 slices American cheese
Milk

Preheat the oven to 375 degrees. Brown the ground beef in a skillet, stirring until crumbly; drain. Season with onion powder, garlic powder, salt and red pepper to taste. Prepare the corn bread mix with the eggs and 1/2 cup milk using the package directions. Stir in the browned ground beef, jalapeño chiles and corn. Line a 9×13-inch baking pan with some of the cheese slices. Break the remaining slices into small pieces and stir them into the ground beef mixture. Thin the mixture with a little milk if it is too thick to stir. Pour the batter into the cheese-lined pan. Bake for 20 to 25 minutes or until a fork inserted in the center comes out clean.

SERVES 10 TO 12

King's Egg Casserole

1 pound Cheddar cheese, shredded	16 green onions, chopped
1 pound Monterey Jack cheese, shredded	Cajun or Creole seasoning to taste
1 pound sliced bacon, diced	12 eggs
1 pound ham, chopped	2 cups all-purpose flour

Preheat the oven to 350 degrees. Combine the Cheddar cheese, Monterey Jack cheese, bacon, ham, green onions and Cajun seasoning in a large mixing bowl and mix well. Beat the eggs and flour together in a bowl. Pour over the cheese mixture and mix well. Pour into a bundt pan coated with nonstick cooking spray. Place the pan on a baking sheet. Bake for 1 hour. Reduce the oven temperature to 325 degrees. Cook for 20 to 30 minutes longer. Cool briefly. Invert the casserole onto a serving dish. Cut into 1/2-inch slices.

SERVES 30

Brunch Egg Casserole

1 pound sliced bacon	3/4 teaspoon seasoned salt
1 pound mushrooms, sliced	Pepper to taste
8 scallions, thinly sliced	Tabasco sauce to taste
12 eggs	33/4 cups (15 ounces) shredded
11/2 cups milk	Monterey Jack cheese

Preheat the oven to 350 degrees. Cook the bacon in a skillet until crisp; drain, reserving 2 tablespoons of the drippings. Crumble the bacon. Add the mushrooms and scallions to the drippings in the skillet. Sauté until the mushrooms are limp. Beat the eggs with the milk, seasoned salt, pepper and Tabasco sauce in a large bowl. Stir in the bacon, mushroom mixture and 3 cups of the cheese. Pour into a greased shallow 2-quart baking dish. Bake, uncovered, for 35 to 40 minutes or until the mixture is set and the top is lightly browned. Sprinkle with the remaining 3/4 cup cheese. Return to the oven and bake until the cheese melts. Serve immediately.

SERVES 12 TO 16

Morning Guests

What to serve a houseful of hungry guests after the "Good mornings" are exchanged and the steaming coffee poured? Brunch Egg Casserole is a versatile, crowd-pleasing recipe that can be offered as part of a hearty country-style breakfast or a more formal bridal brunch; just vary your serving pieces and accompaniments accordingly. A basket of sweet and savory breads and muffins served alongside assorted butters, marmalades, and preserves is a tasty addition to the menu.

Puddin Place Eggs

6 slices Canadian bacon
Shredded mozzarella cheese
6 eggs
Salt and pepper to taste

Heavy cream
Paprika to taste
3 toasted split English muffins

Preheat the oven to 350 degrees. Place a slice of Canadian bacon on the bottom of 6 ramekins coated with nonstick cooking spray. Fill the ramekins with cheese and make a hole in the center of the cheese. Crack an egg into each hole. Season with salt and pepper. Pour enough cream over the egg to barely cover the yolk. Sprinkle with paprika. Bake until the egg is cooked to desired degree of doneness. Scoop out onto toasted English muffin halves.

SERVES 6

Tortilla Brunch Casserole

8 to 10 corn tortillas, cut into
    1/2-inch strips
2 (4-ounce) cans diced green chiles
1 pound bulk pork sausage, cooked and
    drained
2 cups (8 ounces) shredded mixture
    of Cheddar cheese and Monterey
    Jack cheese

8 eggs
1/2 cup milk
1/2 teaspoon salt
1/2 teaspoon garlic salt
1/2 teaspoon cumin
1/2 teaspoon pepper
2 ripe tomatoes, thinly sliced
Paprika to taste

Preheat the oven to 350 degrees. Layer the tortillas, green chiles, sausage and cheese in a greased 9×13-inch baking dish. Combine the eggs, milk, salt, garlic salt, cumin and pepper in a bowl and mix well. Pour over the layers. Arrange the tomato slices over the top and sprinkle with paprika. Bake for 45 minutes or until set.

SERVES 8 TO 10

Soups & Salads

Duck and Andouille Gumbo

Stock
4 (1 1/2-pound) mallards or
   similar ducks
4 1/2 quarts water
3 ribs celery, cut into chunks
1 carrot, cut into halves
15 peppercorns

4 bay leaves
1 1/4 teaspoons salt
1 teaspoon dried thyme
1/4 teaspoon garlic powder
1/4 teaspoon red pepper flakes

Gumbo
3/4 cup all-purpose flour
3/4 cup vegetable oil
2 cups chopped onions
2 cups chopped celery
1 cup chopped green bell pepper
2 carrots, sliced
1 tablespoon chopped garlic
1 pound andouille or other smoked
   sausage, cut into 1/2-inch slices
2/3 cup oyster liquor

1/3 cup port
2 bay leaves
1/2 teaspoon freshly ground
   black pepper
1/4 teaspoon cayenne pepper
2 dozen oysters
1/2 cup chopped green onion tops
1/4 cup chopped fresh parsley
Steamed rice
Filé powder (optional)

For the stock, combine the ducks, water, celery, carrot, peppercorns, bay leaves, salt, thyme, garlic powder and red pepper flakes in a stockpot. Bring to a boil. Reduce the heat and simmer for 3 to 4 hours or until the ducks are tender. Remove the ducks and chop, discarding the skin and bones. Strain the stock into a container, discarding the solids. Chill until the fat has congealed on the stock. Remove the fat and discard.

For the gumbo, brown the flour slowly in the oil in a large heavy pot over medium heat until dark brown, stirring constantly. (This should take about 25 minutes.) Add the onions, celery, bell pepper, carrots and garlic. Cook over medium heat for 5 minutes or until the vegetables are tender. Add 3 quarts of the duck stock, the duck meat, sausage, oyster liquor, port, bay leaves, black pepper and cayenne pepper. Bring to a boil. Reduce the heat and simmer for 1 hour. Stir in the oysters, green onion tops and parsley. Cook for 10 minutes longer. Remove and discard the bay leaves. Ladle the gumbo over steamed rice to serve. Sprinkle with filé powder if desired.

SERVES 10 TO 12

On the Table

Gumbo served in South Louisiana is necessarily accompanied by a scoop of steamed rice and is often sprinkled with chopped green onion tops. Many insist on a side of potato salad—a basic one prepared with just potato, boiled egg, and a touch of mayonnaise and mustard. A basket of lightly toasted French bread, along with hot sauce and filé powder—a thickener made from ground sassafras leaves—are final touches offered at the table.

Shrimp and Okra Gumbo

1/4 cup Savoie's prepared dark roux
2 cups boiling water
1 large onion, chopped
1 green bell pepper, chopped
3 garlic cloves, minced
2 tablespoons vegetable oil
4 cups Smothered Okra, thawed
   (page 131)

4 teaspoons salt
1/4 teaspoon cayenne pepper
8 cups water
2 pounds shrimp, peeled and deveined
1 teaspoon basil
Hot cooked rice
Chicken broth (optional)

Dissolve the prepared dark roux in 2 cups boiling water in a bowl. Sauté the onion, bell pepper and garlic in the oil in a large heavy pot until tender. Add the okra, salt and cayenne pepper. Cook over medium heat until the okra begins to stick to the bottom of the pot. Stir in the dissolved roux and 8 cups water. Bring to a boil. Reduce the heat and simmer for 1 hour. Add the shrimp and basil. Bring to a boil. Reduce the heat and simmer over low heat for 1 hour longer. Ladle over rice to serve.

Note: You may add some chicken broth if the gumbo is too thick.

SERVES 8

Seafood Gumbo

Seasoning Mix

1 bay leaf
2 teaspoons salt
1 teaspoon white pepper
1 teaspoon red pepper

1 teaspoon black pepper
1/2 teaspoon thyme
1/4 teaspoon oregano

Gumbo

1 cup vegetable oil
1 cup all-purpose flour
2 cups chopped onions
1 cup chopped green bell pepper
1 tablespoon minced garlic
5 cups shrimp stock

1 pound andouille sausage, cut into
   1/2-inch slices
1 pound peeled shrimp
1 dozen oysters in liquid
1 pound crab claws
3 cups cooked rice

For the seasoning mix, combine the bay leaf, salt, white pepper, red pepper, black pepper, thyme and oregano in a small bowl and mix well.

For the gumbo, heat the oil in a large heavy pot until it begins to smoke. Whisk in the flour gradually. Cook over medium heat until the roux is dark brown, stirring constantly. Stir in the onions and bell pepper. Cook for 1 minute, stirring constantly. Stir in the seasoning mix and garlic. Cook for 2 to 3 minutes, stirring constantly. Add the shrimp stock. Bring to a boil and simmer for 5 to 10 minutes. Add the sausage. Cook for 15 minutes. Taste and adjust the seasonings if necessary. Reduce the heat to low. Add the shrimp, oysters and crab claws. Cook for 20 to 30 minutes. Let stand for 1 hour. Skim the oil from the surface. Reheat the gumbo slowly. Remove and discard the bay leaf. Ladle over the rice and serve with French bread.

Note: You may make shrimp stock by boiling shrimp shells in water for 1 hour. Strain the stock, discarding the shells.

SERVES 10

South Louisiana Gumbo

Visitors familiar with New Orleans-style gumbo often comment that the gumbos of South Louisiana are markedly different. It is true that South Louisiana gumbo is thinner. This difference is a matter of pride for South Louisianans, who may step forward to offer their opinion on the virtues of their gumbo. Everything is a matter of personal taste, but local cooks proudly suggest that their thin gumbos show off the perfection of their roux and stock.

Corn and Crawfish Bisque

1/2 cup (1 stick) butter
2 tablespoons all-purpose flour
1 onion, chopped
1 green bell pepper, chopped
1 pound crawfish tails
2 cups each half-and-half and milk
1 (14-ounce) can cream-style corn

1 (10-ounce) package frozen corn kernels
1 (10-ounce) can cream of potato soup
1 teaspoon Worcestershire sauce
Salt and pepper to taste
Tabasco sauce to taste
1/3 cup chopped green onions
3 slices provolone cheese, cut into halves

Melt the butter in a soup pot. Whisk in the flour. Cook over medium heat until the mixture is light brown, stirring constantly. Add the onion and bell pepper. Cook until the vegetables are tender. Stir in the crawfish tails, half-and-half, milk, cream-style corn, frozen corn, cream of potato soup, Worcestershire sauce, salt, pepper and Tabasco sauce. Cook for 20 to 30 minutes. Add more milk if the soup is too thick. Add the green onions before serving. Ladle into soup bowls and top each serving with 1/2 slice provolone cheese.

SERVES 6

Crab and Corn Soup

1/2 cup (1 stick) butter
2 tablespoons all-purpose flour
1 large onion, chopped
1 pound white crab meat, shells
    removed and flaked
4 cups evaporated milk
1 (14-ounce) can white
    cream-style corn

1 (11-ounce) can white Shoe Peg corn
1 (15-ounce) can yellow corn
1 (10-ounce) can cream of potato soup
3/4 cup Velveeta cheese
1/2 teaspoon Worcestershire sauce
Tabasco sauce to taste
Salt and pepper to taste
Chicken broth (optional)

Melt the butter in a soup pot over low heat. Whisk in the flour. Add the onion. Sauté until the onion is tender. Stir in the next 11 ingredients. Cook for 30 to 40 minutes. Thin the soup with chicken broth if desired. Ladle into soup bowls and garnish with chopped fresh parsley.

SERVES 8

Special-Occasion Soup

Crab and Corn Soup is a creamy addition to a special-occasion menu—perhaps for a luncheon after a baby's christening or when the extended family gathers for Christmas Eve. Elegant due to the inclusion of crab meat, this is a deceptively simple one-pot dish that requires little cleanup when the party is over. For luncheons or receptions, consider serving small portions of the rich soup in fine demitasse cups.

Chicken Lime Soup

4 chicken breasts
6 (14-ounce) cans reduced-sodium
  chicken broth
1 (14-ounce) can diced tomatoes
1 (4-ounce) can mushrooms, drained
1 red onion, julienned
Juice of 4 or 5 limes
1 tablespoon chopped fresh cilantro
1 tablespoon Tabasco chipotle sauce

1 teaspoon garlic powder
1 teaspoon dried oregano
1 teaspoon salt
1 teaspoon pepper
1 teaspoon paprika
1 large bay leaf
3 ounces Monterey Jack cheese with
  pepper, cubed
2 avocados, cut into chunks

Cook the chicken breasts in the chicken broth in a soup pot until cooked through. Remove the chicken breasts and shred. Add the tomatoes, mushrooms, onion, lime juice, cilantro, chipotle sauce, garlic powder, oregano, salt, pepper, paprika and bay leaf to the broth. Cook for 30 to 60 minutes. Remove and discard the bay leaf. Add the shredded chicken. Ladle into soup bowls and top with the cubed cheese and avocado.

SERVES 6 TO 8

Creamy Vegetable Beef Soup

1 pound stew beef, cubed
3 slices bacon
1 pound ground beef
1 large onion, chopped
1/2 teaspoon chopped garlic
4 carrots, cut into bite-size pieces
1 cup water
2 or 3 potatoes, cubed

1 (14-ounce) can diced tomatoes
1 (14-ounce) can green beans
1 (15-ounce) can yellow corn
1 (11-ounce) can white corn
1 (15-ounce) can peas
Salt, pepper and other desired
  seasonings to taste
8 ounces Velveeta cheese, cubed

Brown the stew beef and bacon in a skillet. Add the ground beef and cook until crumbly; drain. Stir in the onion, garlic, carrots and water. Simmer for 15 minutes. Add the potatoes and simmer for 15 minutes or until tender. Stir in the undrained canned vegetables. Simmer for 1 hour. Add the salt, pepper and seasonings to taste. Add the Velveeta cheese. Cook until the cheese is melted, stirring constantly. Serve immediately.

SERVES 6 TO 8

Taco Soup

2 pounds ground beef
1 envelope taco seasoning
1 envelope fiesta ranch
   salad dressing mix
1 cup water
1 (15-ounce) can kidney beans
1 (15-ounce) can pinto beans
1 (16-ounce) can red beans

1 (15-ounce) can yellow hominy
1 (14-ounce) can cream-style corn
1 (14-ounce) can Mexican-style stewed
   tomatoes
1 (10-ounce) can tomatoes with
   green chiles
1 (4-ounce) can diced green chiles

Brown the ground beef in a soup pot, stirring until crumbly; drain. Stir in the taco seasoning, ranch salad dressing mix and water. Add the undrained kidney beans, undrained pinto beans, undrained red beans, undrained hominy, undrained corn, undrained stewed tomatoes, undrained tomatoes with green chiles and undrained diced green chiles. Simmer for 1 hour.

SERVES 15

Tuscan Soup

3 links spicy Italian sausage,
   casings removed
1 onion, chopped
6 cups chicken broth
3 large potatoes, cut into 1/4-inch slices

1 bunch fresh spinach, chopped
1/4 cup milk
1/2 teaspoon salt
Pinch freshly ground pepper

Brown the sausage and onion in a skillet over medium heat, stirring until the sausage is crumbly; drain. Combine the sausage mixture, chicken broth and potatoes in a soup pot. Cook until the potatoes are tender. Add the spinach. Cook until the spinach is wilted. Remove from the heat. Stir in the milk, salt and pepper.

Note: If using canned chicken broth, taste before adding the salt.

SERVES 4

Ultimate Baked Potato Soup

1 pound sliced bacon, chopped
2 ribs celery, diced
1 onion, chopped
3 garlic cloves, minced
2¹/2 to 3 pounds potatoes, peeled
   and cubed
4 cups chicken stock or chicken broth

3 tablespoons butter
¹/4 cup all-purpose flour
1 cup heavy cream
Salt and pepper to taste
Shredded Cheddar cheese
Chopped green onions
Sour cream

Cook the bacon in a soup pot until crisp; drain, reserving ¹/4 cup of the drippings in the pot. Crumble the bacon. Sauté the celery and onion in the reserved drippings for 5 minutes. Add the garlic. Cook for 3 to 4 minutes. Stir in the bacon, potatoes and enough of the chicken stock to cover the potatoes. Simmer, covered, until the potatoes are tender. Melt the butter in a saucepan over medium heat. Whisk in the flour. Cook for 1 to 2 minutes, stirring constantly. Whisk in the cream. Bring to a boil and cook until thickened, stirring constantly. Stir the cream sauce into the potato mixture. Purée ¹/2 of the soup in a blender or food processor. Stir the puréed soup into the soup pot. Add the salt and pepper. Ladle into soup bowls and top with Cheddar cheese, green onions and sour cream.

SERVES 8

Squash Soup

¹/2 cup (1 stick) butter
1 large onion, chopped
4 cups sliced yellow squash, or
   2 (10-ounce) packages frozen
   sliced yellow squash, thawed
2 potatoes, sliced
2 carrots, sliced
16 ounces chicken stock

16 ounces beef stock
1 tablespoon salt
¹/4 teaspoon cayenne pepper
8 ounces peeled cooked shrimp, or
   8 ounces cooked lobster meat,
   chopped
1 cup milk
Paprika to taste

Melt the butter in a soup pot. Sauté the onion in the butter until tender. Stir in the squash, potatoes, carrots, chicken stock, beef stock, salt and cayenne pepper. Cook, covered, until the vegetables are tender. Add the shrimp. Purée the soup in batches in a blender. Return to the pot. Add the milk. Taste and adjust the seasonings. Ladle into soup bowls and sprinkle with paprika.

SERVES 12

Crawfish Caesar Salad

1 cup chopped onion
1/2 cup chopped green bell pepper
1/2 cup chopped celery
1/4 cup chopped fresh parsley
2 garlic cloves, minced
1/2 cup (1 stick) butter
1/4 cup olive oil
2 bay leaves
1 teaspoon dried oregano
1 teaspoon dried thyme

1 teaspoon Cajun or Creole seasoning,
 or to taste
1/2 cup chardonnay
2 pounds peeled fresh crawfish tails
2 (10-ounce) packages torn romaine
 lettuce
1/2 bottle of Caesar salad dressing
3/4 cup (3 ounces) grated Parmesan or
 Romano cheese
4 ounces Caesar salad croutons

Sauté the onion, bell pepper, celery, parsley and garlic in the butter and olive oil in a large skillet for 10 minutes or until the vegetables are tender. Add the bay leaves, oregano, thyme and Cajun seasoning. Cook over low heat for 5 minutes. Add the chardonnay and simmer for 5 minutes. Stir in the crawfish tails. Cook for 5 to 10 minutes longer. Remove and discard the bay leaves. Toss the lettuce, salad dressing, cheese and croutons in a large bowl. Arrange the salad on individual plates. Spoon the crawfish mixture over the salad, using a slotted spoon to remove excess liquid.

SERVES 6 TO 8

Crab Meat Salad
with Cane Syrup Vinaigrette

1 cup olive oil
1/2 cup cane syrup
1/2 cup balsamic vinegar
1 tablespoon chopped garlic

1/4 cup chopped green onions
Mixed salad greens
1 pound lump crab meat, shells removed
 and flaked

Combine the olive oil, cane syrup, balsamic vinegar, garlic and green onions in a jar and shake well. Arrange salad greens on 12 individual salad plates. Spread the crab meat over the greens. Shake the vinaigrette and drizzle over the salad.

SERVES 12

Dressed Up or Down

The Cane Syrup Vinaigrette used to dress the Crab Meat Salad is a versatile one that will make almost any salad combination a delight. It is especially delicious when topped with salty roasted pecans or toasted pine nuts.

Creole Shrimp Salad

Creole Dressing
2 cups mayonnaise
1/2 cup chili sauce
3 tablespoons Creole mustard
2 garlic cloves, pressed
2 tablespoons Worcestershire sauce

1 tablespoon lemon juice
1 tablespoon paprika
1 teaspoon dry mustard
1 teaspoon Tabasco sauce
Salt to taste

Shrimp Salad
3 pounds fresh deveined peeled shrimp
3 tablespoons liquid crab boil
1 (14-ounce) jar hearts of palm, sliced
3 avocados, diced

1/2 cup chopped red onion
1/2 cup chopped green onions
1/4 cup chopped fresh parsley

For the Creole dressing, combine the mayonnaise, chili sauce, Creole mustard, garlic, Worcestershire sauce, lemon juice, paprika, dry mustard, Tabasco sauce and salt in a bowl and mix well. Chill for several hours before using for the flavors to blend.

For the shrimp salad, bring a large pot of water to a boil. Add the shrimp and liquid crab boil. Cook for 3 to 4 minutes or until the shrimp turn pink; drain. Chill the shrimp until ready to serve. Combine the shrimp and Creole Dressing in a large salad bowl and mix well. Stir the hearts of palm, avocados, red onion, green onions and parsley gently into the shrimp.

SERVES 8

Marinated Shrimp Tortellini

1 1/4 cups olive oil
1/2 cup white vinegar
2/3 cup ketchup
5 garlic cloves, minced
5 teaspoons horseradish
1 tablespoon Dijon mustard
1 tablespoon lemon juice
1 teaspoon Tabasco sauce

1 teaspoon salt
1 teaspoon pepper
3 pounds medium shrimp, cooked
　and peeled
1 pound cheese-filled tortellini, cooked
　and drained
1/2 cup chopped celery

Combine the olive oil, vinegar, ketchup, garlic, horseradish, Dijon mustard, lemon juice, Tabasco sauce, salt and pepper in a large shallow dish and mix well. Add the shrimp, tortellini and celery and toss to coat. Marinate in the refrigerator for at least 24 hours.

SERVES 8 TO 10

Jambalaya Salad

Salad

1 1/3 cups water
2/3 cup uncooked rice
6 slices bacon, crisp-cooked
   and crumbled
8 ounces peeled cooked tiny shrimp

1/2 cup cubed ham
1/2 cup chopped green bell pepper
1/2 cup sliced celery
1/4 cup chopped onion
1 cup chopped tomato

Dressing

3/4 cup Italian salad dressing
1 garlic clove, minced
1 teaspoon chopped fresh thyme

1/4 teaspoon chili powder
1/4 teaspoon Cajun or Creole seasoning
1/4 teaspoon salt

For the salad, combine the water and rice in a saucepan. Bring to a boil. Reduce the heat to low. Cook, covered, for 20 minutes. Combine the rice, bacon, shrimp, ham, bell pepper, celery, onion and tomato in a large salad bowl and mix well.

For the dressing, whisk the Italian salad dressing, garlic, thyme, chili powder, Cajun seasoning and salt together in a small bowl.

To assemble, pour the dressing over the rice mixture and toss to combine. Chill, covered, until serving time.

SERVES 6

Chicken Pesto Pasta Salad

Basil Pesto

2 cups basil leaves
1/4 cup olive oil
2 tablespoons minced garlic

1/2 cup (2 ounces) grated
    Parmesan cheese
1/4 cup Louisiana pecans

Pasta Salad

1 cup mayonnaise
3/4 cup minced celery
4 boneless skinless chicken breasts,
    cooked and cubed (about 3 cups
    cubed chicken)

1 pound penne, cooked and drained
1 cup dried cranberries
1 cup Louisiana pecans, coarsely chopped
1 tablespoon white pepper, or to taste

For the pesto, combine the basil, olive oil, garlic, Parmesan cheese and pecans in a food processor and process until smooth.

For the salad, combine the pesto, mayonnaise and celery in a large salad bowl and mix well. Stir in the chicken, penne, cranberries, pecans and white pepper. Chill until serving time. Serve on a bed of lettuce.

SERVES 10

Oriental Chicken Salad

1 cup mayonnaise
1/4 cup honey
2 tablespoons soy sauce
1 baked, smoked or boiled chicken,
    deboned and chopped

1/2 cup dried cranberries
1/2 cup toasted almonds
1/4 cup chopped green onions
1/2 cup dry chow mein noodles

Combine the mayonnaise, honey and soy sauce in a large bowl and mix well. Fold in the chicken, cranberries and almonds. Fold in the green onions. Chill until serving time. Top with the chow mein noodles. Serve on a bed of lettuce or in avocado halves with crackers or rolls.

SERVES 6 TO 8

Wild Rice and Chicken Salad

1 cup mayonnaise
1/3 cup honey
1/3 cup chopped green onions
2 1/2 tablespoons lemon juice
2 1/2 tablespoons chopped fresh parsley
2 1/2 tablespoons rice wine vinegar or
   balsamic vinegar
1 teaspoon pepper
1/2 teaspoon salt

4 (6-ounce) packages long-grain
   and wild rice mix
5 cups chopped cooked chicken
8 ounces seedless green grapes,
   cut into halves
8 ounces seedless red grapes,
   cut in halves
1 (7-ounce) package sliced almonds,
   toasted

Combine the first 8 ingredients in a bowl and mix well. Cook the rice, using the package directions. Let cool slightly. Combine the rice and chicken in a large serving bowl. Add the dressing and mix well. Chill for at least 6 hours before serving. Stir in the green grapes, red grapes and almonds. Serve with croissants or on lettuce leaves with rolls or crackers.

SERVES 18

Autumn Salad

Dressing
1/2 cup cane syrup
1/4 cup Creole mustard
2 tablespoons apple cider vinegar
Pinch of oregano

Pinch of basil
1 teaspoon Cajun or Creole seasoning
2/3 cup olive oil

Crunchy Candied Pecans
3 tablespoons butter
1/2 cup sugar
1 1/2 cups pecan halves

Salad
6 cups mixed salad greens (green-leaf
   lettuce, Boston lettuce, red-leaf
   lettuce, Romaine)
1/2 cup crumbled blue cheese

For the dressing, combine the cane syrup, mustard, vinegar, oregano, basil and Cajun seasoning in a bowl and mix well. Whisk in the olive oil gradually.

For the pecans, line a baking sheet with foil and butter the foil. Melt the butter in a heavy 10-inch skillet over medium heat. Stir in the sugar and pecan halves. Cook for 4 to 5 minutes or until the sugar melts and turns a rich golden brown, stirring constantly. Remove from the heat. Spread the pecan mixture on the prepared baking sheet. Let cool completely. Break into small pieces.

For the salad, toss the salad greens with the desired amount of dressing in a large salad bowl. Top with the blue cheese and candied pecans.

SERVES 6

Seven-Layer Spinach Salad

1 teaspoon sugar
1 teaspoon salt
1 teaspoon pepper
1 package spinach, washed and dried
1 pound sliced bacon, crisp-cooked
  and crumbled
6 hard-cooked eggs, sliced

1 small head iceberg lettuce, sliced
1 small can water chestnuts, sliced
1 bunch green onions, chopped
1 1/2 cups mayonnaise
1 cup mayonnaise-type salad dressing
8 ounces Swiss cheese, shredded

Mix the sugar, salt and pepper in a bowl. Layer the spinach, bacon, hard-cooked eggs, lettuce, water chestnuts and green onions in a large salad bowl, sprinkling the sugar mixture lightly between each layer. Combine the mayonnaise and salad dressing in a bowl and mix well. Spread over the green onion layer. Sprinkle the cheese evenly over the top. Chill until serving time.

SERVES 6 TO 8

Salade Verte avec Vinaigrette

1 shallot, finely chopped
2 fresh basil leaves, chopped
1 tablespoon white wine vinegar
1 tablespoon lemon juice
1 teaspoon Dijon mustard

1/2 teaspoon sugar
1/3 cup virgin olive oil
Salt and pepper to taste
1 package spring mix salad greens

Combine the shallot, basil, vinegar, lemon juice, Dijon mustard and sugar in a small bowl. Whisk in the olive oil slowly. Add salt and pepper. Drizzle the dressing over the salad greens and toss gently.

SERVES 6

Tabouli

2 cups cracked wheat (bulgur #1)	1 small red or green bell pepper, diced
1 teaspoon salt	4 radishes, sliced into thin rounds and
1/8 teaspoon red pepper	cut into halves
2 large bunches curly parsley, washed	1 cucumber, sliced into rounds and
and dried	quartered (optional)
1/2 cup olive oil	1 teaspoon finely chopped fresh mint, or
1/3 cup lemon juice	1 teaspoon dried mint
1 bunch green onions, finely chopped	1 1/2 teaspoons salt
3 tomatoes, diced	1/8 teaspoon red pepper

Pour the wheat into a large bowl and fill with cold water; drain. Rinse the wheat a second time and pour off excess water, leaving a thin layer of water on top of the wheat. Add 1 teaspoon salt and 1/8 teaspoon red pepper and stir well. Let stand for 1 hour or until the wheat is soft and the water is completely absorbed. Remove the parsley stems and discard. Process the parsley in a food processor until finely chopped. Add the parsley, olive oil and lemon juice to the wheat and mix well. Stir in the green onions, tomatoes, bell pepper, radishes, cucumber, mint, 1 1/2 teaspoons salt and 1/8 teaspoon red pepper. Adjust the seasonings to taste. Add more olive oil or lemon juice if desired. Chill for several hours. Serve on crisp lettuce leaves.

MAKES 12 TO 15 SALAD SERVINGS,
MORE IF USED FOR A COCKTAIL PARTY

Tabouli Tips

Made of bulgur wheat, tabouli is a healthful, colorful salad. Where to find the wheat? Head to your international or health food store for an offering of bulgur wheat in several sizes. Choose #1, or finely ground, for tabouli. As our measurements are a guide, adjust the olive oil and lemon to your taste or to ensure that your dish is not too dry. Spoon the tabouli into crisp lettuce leaves for your guests.

Marinated Green Bean Salad

5 (14-ounce) cans whole green
    beans, drained
2 (14-ounce) cans quartered artichoke
    hearts, drained
1 (8-ounce) can sliced water
    chestnuts, drained
1 cup vegetable oil

1 cup sugar
1/2 cup red wine vinegar
1 tablespoon soy sauce
Salt and pepper to taste
1 cup walnuts or pecans, chopped
1 package ramen noodles, crushed
1/4 cup (1/2 stick) butter

Combine the green beans, artichoke hearts and water chestnuts in a sealable plastic bag. Combine the oil, sugar, vinegar, soy sauce, salt and pepper in a jar and shake well. Pour over the vegetables and seal the bag. Marinate in the refrigerator for 8 to 10 hours. Drain the vegetables in a colander. Sauté the walnuts and ramen noodles in the butter in a skillet until golden brown. Let cool. Combine the vegetables and the walnut mixture in a salad bowl and toss to mix.

SERVES 6 TO 8

Colorful Coleslaw

2 cups shredded white cabbage
2 cups shredded red cabbage
2 cups shredded carrots
1/2 cup minced yellow onion
1/2 to 2/3 cup olive oil
1/4 cup sugar, or 3 packets artificial
    sweetener

1/3 cup red wine vinegar
1 tablespoon Dijon mustard
1 tablespoon caraway seeds
2 splashes of Worcestershire sauce
Salt, black pepper and cayenne pepper
    to taste

Combine the white cabbage, red cabbage, carrots and onion in a large salad bowl. Add the olive oil, sugar, vinegar, Dijon mustard, caraway seeds, Worcestershire sauce, salt, black pepper and cayenne pepper and mix well. Chill until serving time.

SERVES 10 TO 12

Sweet-and-Sour Cucumber Salad

3 English cucumbers
1 tablespoon salt
1/4 cup sugar
1/4 cup white vinegar

1 garlic clove, crushed
1 teaspoon sesame seed oil
1 teaspoon sesame seeds, toasted

Peel the cucumbers at intervals to create a striped pattern. Cut into 1/8-inch slices. Place the cucumber slices in a shallow dish. Sprinkle with the salt and let stand for 20 minutes; drain. Rinse the cucumbers under cold water; drain again. Combine the sugar, vinegar, garlic and sesame seed oil in a serving bowl. Add the cucumbers and toss to coat. Chill until serving time. Sprinkle with the sesame seeds.

SERVES 8

Marinated Vegetable Salad

1/2 cup sugar
1/3 cup vegetable oil
2/3 cup cider vinegar
Salt and pepper to taste
1 (14-ounce) can tiny butter beans, drained, or 1 (10-ounce) package frozen butter beans
1 (14-ounce) can cut green beans, drained

1 (15-ounce) can small green peas, drained
1 (11-ounce) can white Shoe Peg corn
1 small jar chopped pimento
4 ribs celery, diced
1 red onion, finely chopped
1 green bell pepper, finely chopped

Combine the sugar, oil, vinegar, salt and pepper in a shallow dish and mix well. Add the butter beans, green beans, green peas, corn, pimento, celery, onion and bell pepper and stir to mix. Marinate in the refrigerator for 24 hours or longer.

SERVES 6 TO 8

Vegetable Bouquet

1 (14-ounce) can hearts of palm, drained and sliced
1 (14-ounce) can cut green beans, drained
1 (15-ounce) can red kidney beans, drained
1 (15-ounce) can wax beans, drained
1 small can pitted black olives, drained
1 (14-ounce) can artichoke hearts, drained and chopped
1 1/2 cups thin diagonal slices celery
1 red onion, thinly sliced

1 pound mushrooms, sliced
1 (2-ounce) jar chopped pimento
2 tablespoons drained capers
1/2 cup vegetable oil
1/4 cup tarragon vinegar
1/4 cup chopped fresh parsley
1 tablespoon fines herbes
1 1/2 teaspoons MSG
1 1/2 teaspoons salt
1 teaspoon sugar
1/4 teaspoon Tabasco sauce

Combine the hearts of palm, green beans, kidney beans, wax beans, olives, artichoke hearts, celery, onion, mushrooms, pimento and capers in a large sealable container. Combine the oil, vinegar, parsley, fines herbes, MSG, salt, sugar and Tabasco sauce in a jar and shake well. Pour over the vegetables. Marinate in the refrigerator for 8 to 10 hours. Serve chilled or at room temperature.

SERVES 12

Warm Cranberry Salad

2 (16-ounce) cans whole berry cranberry sauce
2 Granny Smith apples, chopped
2 Bosc pears, chopped
1 cup sugar

1/3 cup butter
1/2 cup packed brown sugar
1/4 cup all-purpose flour
1/2 cup pecans, chopped
1/2 cup walnuts, chopped

Preheat the oven to 350 degrees. Combine the cranberry sauce, apples, pears and sugar in a bowl and mix well. Pour into a buttered baking dish. Melt the butter in a small saucepan. Stir in the brown sugar, flour, pecans and walnuts. Spread over the fruit mixture. Bake for 1 hour.

SERVES 8 TO 10

Fruity Spring Mix Salad with Sweet and Hot Vinaigrette

Sweet and Hot Vinaigrette
1/4 cup vegetable oil
1/2 cup balsamic vinegar
2 tablespoons sugar

1/4 teaspoon salt
1/4 teaspoon pepper
1/4 teaspoon hot red pepper sauce

Sugared Almonds
1 cup slivered almonds
1/2 cup sugar

1 teaspoon water

Salad
1 head Bibb or butter lettuce, torn
10 ounces gourmet mixed salad
    greens, torn
2 cups fresh pineapple chunks
2 kiwifruit, sliced

1 (11-ounce) can mandarin oranges,
    drained and chilled
16 green or red seedless grapes, cut into
    halves lengthwise
Poppy Seed Puff Pastry Straws (page 92)

For the vinaigrette, whisk the oil and vinegar together in a bowl, beating for 3 to 4 minutes. Whisk in the sugar, salt, pepper and hot red pepper sauce. Chill for at least 1 hour before serving.

For the sugared almonds, preheat the oven to 300 degrees. Spread the almonds on a foil-lined baking sheet. Bake for 8 to 10 minutes or until light brown. Combine the sugar and water in a heavy saucepan. Bring to a boil over medium heat. Add the almonds and toss to combine. Spread the mixture on foil. Let stand until cool and completely dry. Break into pieces. Store in an airtight container.

For the salad, toss the lettuce, salad greens, pineapple, kiwifruit, oranges and grapes together in a large salad bowl. Drizzle with the vinaigrette just before serving. Sprinkle with the sugared almonds. Serve with Poppy Seed Puff Pastry Straws.

SERVES 8

Celery and Apple Salad

4 ribs celery, chopped
1 crisp red apple, chopped
2 tablespoons mayonnaise
1 tablespoon Dijon mustard

1 teaspoon cider vinegar
1/4 teaspoon sugar
1/4 teaspoon tarragon

Combine the celery, apple, mayonnaise, Dijon mustard, cider vinegar, sugar and tarragon in a bowl and mix well. Chill until serving time.

SERVES 2

Grape Salad

8 ounces cream cheese, softened
3/4 cup sour cream
1/2 cup sugar
1 tablespoon vanilla extract

2 pounds red seedless grapes
2 pounds green seedless grapes
1 cup pecans, toasted
3/4 cup packed brown sugar

Beat the cream cheese with the sour cream, sugar and vanilla in a bowl until smooth. Stir in the grapes. Spoon into a serving dish. Combine the warm toasted pecans with the brown sugar in a bowl and toss to coat. Sprinkle over the grape salad.

SERVES 8 TO 10

Frozen Fruit Salad

2 bananas, mashed
2 tablespoons lemon juice
3/4 cup sugar
1 (8-ounce) can crushed pineapple,
    drained

1/4 cup chopped Bing cherries
1/2 cup chopped nuts
9 ounces whipped topping
1 cup sour cream

Combine the bananas and lemon juice in a large bowl and mix well. Add the sugar, pineapple, cherries, nuts, whipped topping and sour cream and stir well. Pour into a 9×12-inch freezer container. Freeze until firm. Cut into slices to serve.

Note: Freeze the mixture in muffin cups if desired. Place the frozen salads in freezer bags and freeze until needed.

S ERVES 12 TO 15

Orange Sherbet Salad

1 (6-ounce) package orange gelatin
1 cup boiling water
1 pint orange sherbet
1 (8-ounce) can crushed pineapple
1 cup miniature marshmallows

1 (11-ounce) can mandarin
    oranges, drained
1 cup heavy whipping cream, whipped
Chopped pecans (optional)
12 maraschino cherries (optional)

Dissolve the gelatin in the boiling water in a bowl. Stir in the orange sherbet. Chill until partially set. Add the pineapple, marshmallows and oranges. Fold in the whipped cream, pecans and cherries. Chill until firm.

S ERVES 12

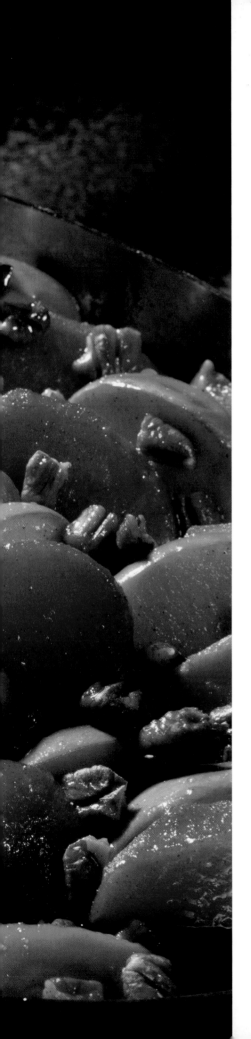

Vegetables &
Sides

Calico Beans

8 ounces bacon, chopped
1 onion, chopped
1/2 green bell pepper, chopped
2 garlic cloves, chopped
1 pound lean ground beef
1/2 cup packed brown sugar
1/2 cup ketchup

2 teaspoons vinegar
1 teaspoon yellow mustard
1 (15-ounce) can red kidney beans or
    pinto beans, drained
1 (15-ounce) can pork and beans
1 (14-ounce) can lima beans, drained
Salt to taste

Cook the bacon in a large skillet until crisp. Add the onion, bell pepper and garlic to the bacon in the skillet and sauté briefly. Add the ground beef. Cook until crumbly, stirring constantly. Simmer for 30 minutes. Combine the brown sugar, ketchup, vinegar and mustard in a small bowl and mix well. Stir into the ground beef mixture. Add the kidney beans, pork and beans, lima beans and salt and stir well. Cook until heated through.

SERVES 8

Green Beans and Potatoes

8 ounces green beans
Salt to taste
3 pounds very small new red potatoes
1/4 cup vermouth
2 tablespoons white wine vinegar
1 large shallot, chopped, or 1/4 cup
    chopped Vidalia onion

1 tablespoon whole-grain mustard or
    Creole mustard
3/4 cup extra-virgin olive oil
2 tablespoons chopped fresh parsley
Pepper to taste

Cook the green beans in boiling salted water in a large saucepan for 4 minutes or until tender-crisp; drain. Submerge the green beans in ice water to stop the cooking process; drain. Dry the green beans. Cut the unpeeled potatoes into halves. Cook in boiling salted water in a large saucepan for 10 to 12 minutes or just until tender; drain. Place the potatoes in a large wide bowl. Sprinkle with the vermouth. Toss gently and let stand for 5 minutes. Combine the vinegar, shallot and mustard in a small bowl. Whisk in the olive oil gradually. Pour the dressing over the potatoes and toss gently. Cool completely. Stir in the green beans, parsley, salt and pepper. Chill, covered, until serving time. Serve cold or at room temperature.

SERVES 6 TO 8

Carrots Supreme Casserole

8 cups sliced carrots
Salt to taste
1 small onion, chopped
1 tablespoon butter
1 (10-ounce) can cream of
  mushroom soup

1 (4-ounce) can mushroom stems and
  pieces, drained
1/2 cup (2 ounces) grated
  Parmesan cheese
1 cup soft bread crumbs

Preheat the oven to 350 degrees. Cook the carrots in boiling salted water in a saucepan until tender; drain. Sauté the onion in the butter in a large skillet until tender. Add the carrots, soup, mushrooms and cheese and mix well. Pour into a greased 2 1/2-quart baking dish. Sprinkle with the bread crumbs. Bake, uncovered, for 30 to 35 minutes or until heated through.

SERVES 6

Carrot Beignets

2 pounds carrots, cut into small chunks
Salt to taste
2 eggs
1 tablespoon vanilla extract

2 cups sugar
1 teaspoon ground cinnamon
2 1/2 cups (or more) self-rising flour
Vegetable oil for deep-frying

Cook the carrots in boiling salted water just until tender; drain. Mash the carrots in a large bowl. Beat in the eggs, vanilla, sugar and cinnamon. Stir in the flour. Add more flour as needed to make a soft dough. Drop by tablespoonfuls into 350-degree oil. Fry until golden on both sides. Drain on paper towels.

MAKES 2 DOZEN

Sweet or Savory

Visitors to Louisiana are familiar with our famous beignets, plump pillows of fried dough served piping hot with a generous coating of confectioners' sugar. What a treat with café au lait! Luckily, beignets are not reserved for dessert, but come in a variety of sweet and savory choices. Carrot Beignets are a variation that not only tastes great alone, but will also make an interesting addition to your family's next fish fry.

Carrots in Orange Sauce

1 (16-ounce) package small carrots
1/2 cup orange juice
1/2 cup sugar
1 tablespoon cornstarch

1 tablespoon orange rind, grated
1 teaspoon salt
2 tablespoons butter

Preheat the oven to 350 degrees. Steam the carrots until tender; drain. Combine the orange juice, sugar, cornstarch, orange rind and salt in a small saucepan. Cook over low heat until blended, stirring constantly. Stir in the butter. Combine the carrots and orange sauce in a baking dish. Bake, covered, for 30 minutes. Garnish with chopped fresh parsley.

SERVES 4 TO 6

Corn Maque Choux

3 slices bacon, cut into 1-inch pieces
1/2 cup chopped onion
1/4 cup chopped green bell pepper
1 garlic clove, minced
1 (10-ounce) can tomatoes with green chiles, drained

1 (12-ounce) can whole-kernel corn, undrained
3 (12-ounce) cans whole-kernel corn, drained
2 tablespoons butter

Cook the bacon in a skillet until crisp; drain off excess drippings. Add the onion, bell pepper and garlic. Sauté until the onion is tender. Add the tomatoes with green chiles. Cook for 2 minutes. Process the undrained corn in a blender until smooth. Add to the tomato mixture. Stir in the drained corn and butter. Cook over medium heat until the mixture thickens, stirring frequently.

SERVES 6 TO 8

Corn Casserole

1/2 cup each chopped onion and celery
3 tablespoons butter
2 (11-ounce) cans white Shoe Peg corn
1 (15-ounce) can French-style green
   beans, drained
2 cups (8 ounces) shredded sharp
   Cheddar cheese

2 cups sour cream
1 (10-ounce) can cream of
   mushroom soup
Salt and pepper to taste
1/4 cup (1/2 stick) butter, melted
1 roll butter crackers, crushed

Preheat the oven to 400 degrees. Sauté the onion and celery in 3 tablespoons butter in a skillet until tender. Remove to a large mixing bowl. Stir in the corn, green beans, cheese, sour cream, soup, salt and pepper. Pour into a 10×13-inch baking dish. Combine the melted butter and crackers in a small bowl, stirring until crumbly. Sprinkle evenly over the top. Bake for 10 minutes. Reduce the oven temperature to 350 degrees. Bake for 20 minutes or until hot and bubbly.

SERVES 10 TO 12

Smothered Okra

5 pounds okra, chopped
1 large onion, chopped
1 green bell pepper, chopped

1 (8-ounce) can tomato sauce
1 cup vegetable oil
Salt and pepper to taste

Preheat the oven to 450 degrees. Combine the okra, onion, bell pepper, tomato sauce and oil in a large roasting pan and mix well. Reduce the oven temperature to 350 degrees. Bake, covered, for 1 hour, stirring 2 or 3 times during the baking. Uncover the pan. Bake for 2 hours longer. Season with salt and pepper when ready to use.

MAKES 4 PINTS

Planning for Gumbo Season

A favorite when served with homegrown tomatoes, Smothered Okra is a traditional accompaniment to Sunday dinner's hearty roast. Plan ahead by making an extra batch for use in future gumbos. Simply prepare the dish according to the recipe, divide into 2-cup portions, and freeze. As freezing may distort the seasonings, avoid adding any salt or pepper to the okra. When your family is ready for Shrimp and Okra Gumbo (page 107), you will be one step ahead.

Okra Delight

1 onion, chopped
1/3 cup olive oil
1 pound okra, chopped
1 (14-ounce) can chicken broth
1 tablespoon ketchup

1/2 teaspoon vinegar
1/4 teaspoon Cajun or Creole seasoning
1/2 teaspoon salt
1/4 teaspoon pepper
1/4 teaspoon Worcestershire sauce

Sauté the onion in the olive oil in a large skillet until tender. Stir in the remaining ingredients. Cook over medium heat for 30 minutes, adding water if the mixture becomes too thick.

SERVES 5 TO 6

Vidalia Onion Pie

2 pounds Vidalia onions,
  coarsely chopped
1/2 cup (1 stick) butter
3 eggs, beaten
1 cup sour cream

1/2 cup (2 ounces) grated
  Parmesan cheese
1/4 teaspoon salt
1/2 teaspoon white pepper
1 unbaked (9-inch) pie shell

Preheat the oven to 450 degrees. Sauté the onions in the butter in a large skillet until the onions are tender. Drain the onions. Combine the eggs, sour cream, cheese, salt and white pepper in a bowl and mix well. Fold in the onions. Pour into the pie shell. Bake for 20 minutes. Reduce the oven temperature to 350 degrees. Bake for 20 minutes longer.

SERVES 8

Camp Potatoes

1 package Trahan's mixed smoked
  sausage, cut into 1/2-inch pieces
2 onions, chopped
1 green bell pepper, chopped
6 potatoes, diced

Cajun or Creole seasoning to taste
2 tablespoons minced garlic
1 bunch fresh parsley, chopped
1 bunch green onions, chopped

Sauté the sausage, onions and bell pepper in a large skillet or soup pot until the sausage is browned. Add the potatoes and enough water to reach just below the top of the ingredients. Stir in the Cajun seasoning and garlic. Bring to a boil. Reduce the heat and simmer until the potatoes are tender and the water has evaporated, stirring frequently. Stir in the parsley and green onions.

SERVES 4 TO 5

Hash Brown Casserole

1 (2-pound) package frozen hash
   brown potatoes, thawed
1/2 cup chopped onion
10 ounces shredded mild Cheddar cheese
2 cups sour cream

1 (10-ounce) can cream of chicken soup
1 teaspoon salt
1/2 teaspoon pepper
2 cups cornflakes
1/2 cup (1 stick) butter, melted

Preheat the oven to 350 degrees. Combine the hash brown potatoes and the next 6 ingredients in a large bowl and mix well. Pour into a large greased baking dish. Combine the cornflakes and melted butter in a small bowl and mix well. Spread over the top. Bake for 45 minutes.

SERVES 8 TO 10

Spinach la Louisiane

1 cup (2 sticks) butter
1 cup chopped onion
1 cup chopped celery
1 cup chopped green bell pepper
1/4 cup minced garlic
2 cups finely chopped tasso (optional)
1 cup all-purpose flour
7 cups half-and-half

1 cup diced fresh tomatoes, or
   1 (14-ounce) can diced tomatoes,
   drained
8 ounces Mexican Velveeta cheese, cubed
Salt and pepper to taste
Tabasco sauce to taste.
4 (10-ounce) packages frozen spinach,
   thawed and squeezed dry

Preheat the oven to 375 degrees. Melt the butter in a large skillet or saucepan over medium-high heat. Add the onion, celery, bell pepper, garlic and tasso. Sauté for 10 minutes or until the vegetables are tender. Add the flour slowly. Cook for 5 minutes, stirring constantly. Add the half-and-half. Cook until the mixture has thickened, stirring constantly. Stir in the tomatoes and cheese. Cook over low heat for 10 minutes or until the cheese is melted, stirring constantly. Season with salt, pepper and Tabasco sauce. Add the spinach and mix well. Pour into a 9×13-inch baking dish coated with nonstick cooking spray. Bake for 30 minutes.

SERVES 12

An Appetizing Side

In addition to serving as a spicy vegetable selection for the holiday table, Spinach la Louisiane can also be served as a warm hors d'oeuvre for your seasonal cocktail parties. Simply serve in a chafing dish accompanied by pastry shells, garlic-flavored melba toast, or petite puff pastry cups. Because only a small spoonful is needed for each serving, one batch of this recipe will make approximately seventy-five appetizer servings.

Spinach Cheese Bake

1 (6-ounce) package yellow
    corn bread mix
2 eggs, beaten
1 cup sour cream
1 (10-ounce) package frozen chopped
    spinach, thawed and squeezed dry

1 (10-ounce) can French onion soup
1/2 cup (1 stick) butter or
    margarine, melted
1/2 cup (2 ounces) shredded
    Cheddar cheese

Preheat the oven to 350 degrees. Combine the corn bread mix, eggs, sour cream, spinach, onion soup and butter in a large bowl and mix well. Pour into a greased 8×12-inch baking dish. Bake for 25 minutes. Top with the cheese. Bake for 5 minutes longer.

SERVES 8

Broiled Stuffed Tomatoes

3 tomatoes, cut into halves
Salt and pepper to taste
1 (10-ounce) package frozen chopped
    spinach, cooked and drained
3 ounces cream cheese, softened

1/2 cup (1 stick) butter or
    margarine, melted
1 tablespoon lemon juice
Grated Parmesan cheese to taste

Preheat the broiler. Place the tomato halves on a broiler pan. Sprinkle lightly with salt and pepper. Combine the spinach, cream cheese, butter and lemon juice in a bowl and mix well. Spoon on top of the tomato halves. Sprinkle with Parmesan cheese. Broil until the topping is hot and lightly browned.

SERVES 6

Tomato Pie

4 tomatoes, peeled and sliced
Salt to taste
10 fresh basil leaves, chopped
1/2 cup chopped green onions
1 baked (9-inch) deep-dish pie shell
Pepper to taste

1 cup (4 ounces) shredded
    mozzarella cheese
1 cup (4 ounces) shredded
    Cheddar cheese
1 cup mayonnaise

Preheat the oven to 350 degrees. Place the tomato slices in a single layer in a colander. Sprinkle with salt. Let stand for 10 minutes to allow the juices to drain. Layer the tomato slices, basil and green onions in the pie shell. Sprinkle with salt and pepper. Combine the mozzarella cheese, Cheddar cheese and mayonnaise in a bowl and mix well. Spread over the green onion layer. Bake for 30 minutes or until lightly browned. Serve warm.

SERVES 8

Sweet Potatoes au Gratin

3 pounds sweet potatoes
3 Granny Smith apples, peeled and cut
    into 1/2-inch-thick wedges
1/4 cup lemon juice
1 1/2 cups chopped pecans

1/2 cup (1 stick) butter
1/2 cup packed light brown sugar
1/2 cup honey
2 tablespoons dark rum
1/2 teaspoon ground cinnamon

Preheat the oven to 400 degrees. Bake the sweet potatoes for 45 minutes or until tender. Cool completely. Peel the sweet potatoes and slice. Toss the apples with the lemon juice in a bowl. Arrange the sweet potato slices and apple wedges alternately with the slices overlapping in a single layer in a buttered baking dish. Sprinkle with the pecans. Combine the butter, brown sugar, honey, rum and cinnamon in a saucepan. Cook over medium heat until the sugar dissolves, stirring constantly. Spoon over the sweet potatoes and apples. Bake for 30 minutes, basting occasionally.

SERVES 4 TO 6

A Simple Treat

The fall harvest of South Louisiana sweet potatoes and yams is worth the year's wait. Due to their natural sugars, these dark orange beauties require no elaborate preparation. In fact, sweet potatoes roasted until soft and served simply with salt and pepper are a cold-weather favorite. However, the sweet potato is also creatively used in breads, side dishes, and desserts. Sweet Potatoes au Gratin is a tasty example.

Sweet Potato Casserole

2 large cans sweet potatoes, mashed
2 eggs, beaten
1/2 cup (1 stick) butter or margarine,
    softened
1/3 cup milk
1/4 cup granulated sugar
1 teaspoon vanilla extract

1/2 teaspoon ground cinnamon
1 1/2 cups chopped pecans
1 cup packed brown sugar
1/2 cup (1 stick) butter, melted
1/2 cup all-purpose flour
3 tablespoons flaked coconut,
    or to taste

Preheat the oven to 350 degrees. Combine the sweet potatoes, eggs, softened butter, milk, granulated sugar, vanilla and cinnamon in a mixing bowl. Beat until smooth. Pour into a buttered 9×13-inch baking dish. Combine the pecans, brown sugar, melted butter, flour and coconut in a bowl and mix well. Spread over the sweet potato mixture. Bake, uncovered, for 30 minutes.

SERVES 15

Roasted Vegetables

2 yellow squash, sliced
2 zucchini, sliced
1 red bell pepper, julienned
8 ounces mushrooms, sliced

3 or 4 garlic cloves, sliced
1/2 cup olive oil
Cajun or Creole seasoning to taste

Preheat the oven to 400 degrees. Combine the yellow squash, zucchini, bell pepper, mushrooms, garlic and olive oil in a large shallow baking pan, turning to coat the vegetables evenly with the oil. Sprinkle with Cajun seasoning. Bake for 45 to 60 minutes, stirring occasionally.

SERVES 3 TO 4

A Meatless Meal

Colorful and nutritious, Roasted Vegetables are a worthy side to steak, pork roast, or grilled fish. For a vegetarian meal, toss the cooked vegetables with your favorite pasta and top with delicate slivers of Parmigiano-Reggiano. Serve with a crisp green salad, toasted French bread, and a chilled chardonnay.

Sausage Corn Bread Dressing

1 pound hot bulk pork sausage
1 pound mild bulk pork sausage
1 (14-ounce) package chopped Creole
  seasoning blend (mixture of onions,
  green bell peppers, celery, garlic
  and parsley)
1 (4-ounce) can sliced mushrooms,
  drained

3 (6-ounce) packages corn bread mix,
  prepared and baked using the
  package directions
1 (10-ounce) can cream of
  mushroom soup
2 (12-ounce) cans evaporated milk
Pinch of sage

Preheat the oven to 350 degrees. Brown the hot sausage and mild sausage in a skillet, stirring until crumbly; drain, reserving some of the drippings. Cook the Creole seasoning in the reserved drippings in a large skillet until the onions are tender. Stir in the mushrooms. Cook for 4 to 5 minutes longer. Crumble the corn bread into the vegetable mixture. Add the sausage and mix well. Stir in the soup. Add the evaporated milk and sage and mix well. Pour into a greased 11×13-inch baking dish. Bake at 350 degrees for 30 minutes.

SERVES 15

Seafood Corn Bread Dressing

1/2 cup chopped onion
3 tablespoons vegetable oil or butter
1 cup mixed chopped red and green
  bell pepper
1/2 cup chopped celery
1 garlic clove, chopped
1 (10-ounce) can cream of shrimp soup
1 1/4 cups water
1 cup chopped peeled uncooked shrimp

1 cup crab meat
1 cup oysters, drained (optional)
Cajun or Creole seasoning to taste
1 package corn bread mix,
  prepared and baked using the
  package directions
1/2 cup chopped green onions
1 cup (4 ounces) shredded jalapeño
  cheese

Preheat the oven to 350 degrees. Sauté the onion in the oil in a large skillet until the onion is tender. Add the bell pepper, celery and garlic. Sauté for 5 minutes or until the vegetables are tender. Stir in the soup, water, shrimp, crab meat, oysters and Cajun seasoning. Bring to a boil over medium heat, stirring constantly. Crumble the corn bread into the seafood mixture. Stir in the green onions and cheese. Spoon into a greased 9×13-inch baking dish. Bake for 30 to 40 minutes or until golden brown.

SERVES 10 TO 12

Oyster Rice Dressing

3 (1-pound) containers frozen dressing
  mix, thawed
4 cups chicken broth or beef broth

6 cups cooked rice
6 dozen oysters, drained

Combine the dressing and 2 cups of the broth in a large heavy skillet or roasting pan. Stir in the rice. Cook over medium heat for 20 minutes, stirring occasionally. Add the remaining 2 cups broth. Cook over low heat for 1 hour, stirring occasionally. Fold in the oysters. Cook for 10 to 20 minutes or until the edges of the oysters curl.

SERVES 15 TO 20

Jalapeño Cheese Grits

1 tablespoon butter
1 red bell pepper, chopped (1 1/2 cups)
1 yellow bell pepper, chopped (1 1/2 cups)
1 1/2 tablespoons minced seeded
  jalapeño chiles
1 garlic clove, minced

3 cups chicken stock
1 cup heavy cream
1 cup quick-cooking grits
1 1/2 cups (6 ounces) shredded Monterey
  Jack cheese with pepper
Salt and pepper to taste

Melt the butter in a skillet over medium-high heat. Add the red bell pepper, yellow bell pepper, jalapeño chiles and garlic. Sauté for 5 minutes or until the bell peppers are tender. Combine the chicken stock and cream in a large saucepan. Add the grits in a thin stream, whisking constantly. Whisk for 6 minutes or until the grits are cooked and the mixture has thickened. Add the bell pepper mixture and cheese. Cook until the cheese melts, stirring constantly. Season with salt and pepper.

SERVES 6

Changing the Routine

Ask any Southerner to describe his or her typical breakfast, and grits are likely to be mentioned. Jalapeño Cheese Grits change the breakfast routine just a bit and make a tasty addition to a breakfast or brunch buffet. Although satisfying alone, these grits also serve as a hearty base to Shrimp Grillades (page 151).

Creamy Lemon Rice

1/2 cup (1 stick) unsalted butter
2 cups uncooked long grain white rice
Grated zest of 2 lemons
3 cups chicken broth, boiling
1 teaspoon salt

2 tablespoons fresh lemon juice
1 cup heavy cream
Freshly ground pepper to taste
1 tablespoon chopped fresh parsley
  (optional)

Melt the butter in a saucepan over low heat. Stir in the rice and lemon zest. Cook for 5 minutes or until the rice is opaque, stirring constantly. Add the broth and salt. Simmer, covered, for 20 minutes or until the liquid is absorbed. Stir in the lemon juice. Add the cream slowly, stirring constantly. Cook over low heat for 5 minutes or until the cream is absorbed, stirring constantly. Remove from the heat and stir in the parsley.

SERVES 8 TO 10

Festive Rice and Sausage

1 pound smoked sausage, sliced
1 onion, sliced
1 tablespoon olive oil
1 green bell pepper, sliced
1 red bell pepper, sliced

1 yellow bell pepper, sliced
1 (14-ounce) can Italian-style diced
  tomatoes
Hot cooked rice

Sauté the sausage and onion in the olive oil in a large skillet or Dutch oven for 2 to 3 minutes. Add the bell peppers. Sauté for 5 to 6 minutes. Add the tomatoes. Cook until heated through. Serve over rice.

SERVES 6

A Pantry Staple

The importance of rice on the South Louisiana table cannot be overstated. Whether simply steamed or as a component in gumbo, étouffée, jambalaya, or dressing, rice is a given on the menu. Our love of rice is undoubtedly a result of rice production's importance to the area economy. What type of rice should you choose? Many cooks reach for Louisiana-grown long grain rice, finding that it offers the perfect texture for local recipes.

Seafood & Poultry

Easy Salmon Cakes

1 (2- to 3-pound) salmon fillet
1/4 cup orange juice
1 (3-ounce) bag cracklings, crushed
1 cup minced celery
1/4 cup minced sweet onion

1 teaspoon snipped fresh dill weed
2 eggs, lightly beaten
1 cup mayonnaise
Juice of 1/2 lemon
Salt and white pepper to taste

Place the fish skin side down in a poaching pan. Add water to cover the fish. Pour the orange juice over the fish. Poach for 9 minutes per inch of thickness, keeping the liquid just below boiling. Remove the pan from the heat. Let stand until cool. Discard the liquid. Chill the salmon thoroughly. Preheat the oven to 450 degrees. Flake the salmon into a mixing bowl, discarding the skin and bones. Add the cracklings, celery, onion and dill weed and mix well. Stir in the eggs. Fold in the mayonnaise and lemon juice. Season with salt and white pepper. Shape into cakes 3 inches round and 1 1/2 inches thick. Place on a baking sheet. Bake for 20 minutes

Note: You may wrap the cakes in waxed paper and freeze until ready to bake if desired.

SERVES 6 TO 8

Deep-Fried Fish

4 to 6 fish fillets, rinsed and dried
2 cups buttermilk
2 cups cornmeal

1 cup all-purpose flour
Cajun or Creole seasoning to taste
Vegetable oil for deep-frying

Marinate the fish fillets in the buttermilk in a shallow dish in the refrigerator for 1 hour. Combine the cornmeal, flour and Cajun seasoning in a large sealable plastic bag and mix well. Remove 1 fillet at a time from the buttermilk. Drop into the cornmeal mixture in the bag and shake well to coat. Fry the fillets 2 or 3 at a time in 375-degree oil in a deep fryer until golden brown on both sides; drain on paper towels.

SERVES 4 TO 6

Frying Tips

Accompany your fish fry with Fried Mushrooms and Fried Zucchini. The fish fry batter doubles as a vegetable batter as well. Fry these "extras" *before* the fish, as they impart less flavor to the oil. Choose fresh canola, corn, peanut, or safflower oil, as they fry well at higher temperatures with less burning. Use a pan featuring a base wider than the burner to prevent splatters from reaching the heat source. Fill the pot only halfway with oil to leave room for rising bubbles. Fish or vegetables should float freely; overcrowding will reduce the temperature and result in excess oil absorption. To drain, use platters layered with paper bags and topped with paper towels.

Grilled Salmon with Homemade Dill Mayonnaise

Homemade Dill Mayonnaise

1 egg
1 tablespoon white vinegar
2 tablespoons yellow mustard
1 teaspoon salt

2 cups canola oil, or
    blended canola and corn oil
1 tablespoon dried dill weed
1/2 tablespoon red pepper flakes

Salmon

1 large salmon fillet, or
    4 to 6 salmon steaks
1/2 cup dry vermouth

1 to 2 tablespoons dried dill weed
Cajun or Creole seasoning to taste
3 tablespoons butter, broken into pieces

For the mayonnaise, combine the egg, vinegar, yellow mustard and salt in a food processor fitted with a steel blade. Process for 1 minute. Add 1/2 of the canola oil very slowly, processing constantly. Scrape down the side of the bowl with a spatula. Add the remaining canola oil slowly, processing constantly until smooth and creamy. Add the dill weed and red pepper flakes. Process for 15 seconds longer. Store the mayonnaise in a tightly covered jar for up to 2 weeks.

For the salmon, marinate the salmon flesh side down in the vermouth in a shallow bowl for 30 minutes. Turn the salmon flesh side up. Sprinkle with the dill weed and Cajun seasoning. Dot with the butter. Preheat the grill. Place the salmon skin side down on a grill rack coated with nonstick cooking spray. Close the grill cover. Grill over medium-hot coals for 25 to 30 minutes or until the fish flakes easily.

To serve, remove the salmon to a serving platter. Cut the salmon into serving-size pieces, discarding the skin. Serve with a dollop of the mayonnaise. Garnish with fresh dill weed.

Note: If you are concerned about using raw eggs, use eggs pasteurized in their shells, which are sold at some specialty food stores.

SERVES 4 TO 6

Speckled Trout with Vegetables

1 green bell pepper, cut into
   1/8-inch slices
1 tablespoon margarine
1 lemon, cut into 1/8-inch slices
1 tomato, cut into 1/8-inch slices

4 trout fillets
Cajun or Creole seasoning to taste
Pinch of onion powder
1 tablespoon paprika
Margarine

Sauté the bell pepper in 1 tablespoon margarine in a skillet until partially cooked. Layer the lemon and tomato slices over the bell pepper. Cook for 2 minutes without stirring. Remove from the heat. Season the trout fillets with Cajun seasoning, onion powder and paprika. Sauté the fillets in a little margarine in a skillet over medium heat until golden brown on both sides. Remove to a serving dish. Spoon the vegetables over the fish.

SERVES 2

Seafood au Gratin

8 ounces crawfish tails
8 ounces peeled cooked shrimp
8 ounces lump crab meat, shells removed
2 garlic cloves, minced
2 tablespoons butter
1/2 cup chicken broth
1 tablespoon liquid crab boil

1/2 teaspoon Cajun or Creole seasoning
3/4 cup milk
1 (8-ounce) jar Alfredo sauce
12 ounces Velveeta cheese, cubed
8 ounces noodles, cooked
2 cups (8 ounces) shredded
   mozzarella cheese

Preheat the oven to 350 degrees. Sauté the crawfish tails, shrimp, crab meat and garlic in the butter in a skillet until the seafood is heated through. Stir in the chicken broth, liquid crab boil, Cajun seasoning, milk, Alfredo sauce and Velveeta cheese. Cook over medium-low heat until the cheese melts, stirring constantly. Spread the noodles in a greased 9×13-inch baking dish. Pour the seafood sauce over the noodles. Top with the mozzarella cheese. Bake until the mozzarella cheese melts.

SERVES 8 TO 10

Crawfish Étouffée

2 cups (4 sticks) butter
5 cups chopped onions
2 cups chopped celery
1 cup chopped green bell pepper
1 cup chopped red bell pepper
4 teaspoons salt
1 1/2 teaspoons cayenne pepper

1/4 cup all-purpose flour
1/2 cup cold water
4 pounds crawfish tails, deveined
1 cup hot water
1 bunch green onions, chopped
Hot cooked rice

Melt the butter in a large saucepan or Dutch oven. Add the onions, celery, green bell pepper and red bell pepper. Sauté over medium heat until the onion is translucent. Add the salt and cayenne pepper. Reduce the heat to low and simmer for 1 hour, stirring occasionally. Dissolve the flour in 1/2 cup cold water. Stir the flour mixture into the vegetables. Cook for 3 minutes or until thickened, stirring constantly. Add the crawfish and 1 cup hot water. Simmer over low heat for 15 to 20 minutes. Add more water if mixture is too thick. Stir in the green onions. Serve over rice.

SERVE 6 TO 8

Easy Crawfish Fettuccini

1 to 2 pounds crawfish tails
Butter
1 (14-ounce) package frozen chopped
  seasoning blend (chopped onions,
  bell peppers and parsley), thawed
3/4 cup (1 1/2 sticks) butter

1/4 cup all-purpose flour
1 pound Mexican Velveeta cheese,
  cut into small pieces
Half-and-half
Salt and pepper to taste
1 pound fettuccini, cooked

Sauté the crawfish tails in some butter in a skillet until cooked through. Sauté the seasoning blend in 3/4 cup butter in a large skillet over medium heat until tender. Stir in the flour. Cook for 15 minutes, stirring constantly. Add the crawfish and cheese. Cook until the cheese melts, stirring constantly. Add enough half-and-half gradually to reach the desired consistency. Season with salt and pepper. Pour over the cooked pasta in a bowl and toss to coat.

SERVES 8

A Time-Saver

South Louisiana cooks know a convenience item when they see it. As many regional dishes begin with chopped onions, green peppers, and celery, busy cooks look to the produce section for a pre-chopped blend of these ingredients. Some blends include garlic and parsley as well. Frozen chopped onions are another convenience item used by many experienced cooks. When making substitutions, experiment with these products to ensure that the balance of ingredients is as desired for the dish.

Crawfish Enchilada Casserole

3/4 cup (1 1/2 sticks) butter, melted
1/4 cup all-purpose flour
3/4 cup diced onion
1/2 cup diced green bell pepper
2 pounds crawfish tails, rinsed and
    drained
3/4 cup drained diced tomatoes with
    green chiles

1/3 cup chicken broth
4 cups heavy cream
1 tablespoon Cajun or Creole seasoning
1 teaspoon each sugar, chili powder and
    garlic powder
1 pound Velveeta cheese, shredded
12 to 16 corn tortillas

Preheat the oven to 350 degrees. Melt 1/4 cup of the butter in a saucepan. Stir in the flour. Cook to form a blond roux, stirring constantly. Melt the remaining butter in a heavy saucepan or Dutch oven. Add the onion and bell pepper. Sauté until tender. Add the crawfish, tomatoes with green chiles and chicken broth. Sauté for 5 minutes. Stir in the cream, Cajun seasoning, sugar, chili powder and garlic powder. Bring to a boil and stir in the blond roux. Cook for 15 minutes or until thickened, stirring constantly. Fold in 1/2 of the Velveeta cheese. Cook until melted, stirring constantly. Alternate layers of the tortillas and crawfish mixture in a 10×13-inch baking pan coated with nonstick cooking spray, beginning with the tortillas and ending with the crawfish mixture. Top with the remaining Velveeta cheese. Bake for 20 minutes. Broil for 5 minutes longer or until the cheese is melted. Let stand for 15 minutes before serving.

SERVES 8

Crab Meat Étouffée

1 onion, chopped
1 green bell pepper, chopped
1 rib celery, chopped
1 tablespoon chopped fresh parsley
1/4 cup olive oil
2 tablespoons all-purpose flour
1 (10-ounce) can beef broth
1 pound lump crab meat

2 fresh basil leaves, chopped
1/4 teaspoon chopped fresh thyme
1 tablespoon Worcestershire sauce
1/4 teaspoon Tabasco sauce
1 teaspoon salt
1/4 teaspoon pepper
1/3 cup water
2 cups rice, cooked

Sauté the onion, bell pepper, celery and parsley in the olive oil in a large saucepan or Dutch oven until tender but not brown. Stir in the flour. Cook for 5 minutes, stirring constantly. Stir in the beef broth gradually. Cook until thickened, stirring constantly. Stir in the crab meat, basil, thyme, Worcestershire sauce, Tabasco sauce, salt, pepper and water. Cook just until heated through. Serve over the rice.

SERVES 8

Lump Crab Meat Casserole

1 large white onion, finely chopped
3 ribs celery, finely chopped
1/2 cup (1 stick) butter
1/4 cup all-purpose flour
2 cups heavy cream

Salt and white pepper to taste
2 pounds lump crab meat,
  shells removed
Velveeta cheese, shredded

Preheat the oven to 350 degrees. Sauté the onion and celery in the butter in a large skillet until tender but not brown. Stir in the flour. Add the cream gradually. Cook until thickened, stirring constantly. Add the salt and white pepper and mix well. Divide the crab meat among 8 individual baking dishes. Spoon the sauce over the crab meat. Sprinkle with cheese. Bake for 20 to 30 minutes or until cooked through.

SERVES 8

Oak Grove Oyster Pie

2 green bell peppers, chopped
2 onions, chopped
4 ribs celery, chopped
6 garlic cloves, chopped
1/2 cup (1 stick) butter
2 tablespoons prepared roux

2 quarts oysters, drained
Salt-free Creole seasoning to taste
Lemon pepper and garlic salt to taste
4 refrigerator pie pastries
Cracker crumbs
Half-and-half

Preheat the oven to 350 degrees. Sauté the bell peppers, onions, celery and garlic in the butter in a skillet until the onions are tender. Add the roux and cook until melted, stirring constantly. Stir in the oysters. Cook for 15 minutes. Season with Creole seasoning, lemon pepper and garlic salt. Unfold the pastries. Line 2 pie plates with 2 of the pastries. Spread a layer of cracker crumbs in the pastry shells. Spoon the oyster filling over the crumbs. Sprinkle cracker crumbs over the filling. Top with the remaining pie pastries, sealing the edges and cutting vents. Brush the tops with half-and-half. Bake for 40 minutes or until golden brown.

MAKES 2 PIES

Our Little Secret

Do as many South Louisiana cooks do to save time: use prepared roux. Authentically produced by several Louisiana companies, prepared roux is available through mail order if you can't find it in your area. Prepared roux can be more concentrated than homemade roux, so you may need to taste your gumbo a time or two and adjust the amount of roux you add. With those tasty tests, you will soon be an efficient Cajun cook!

Louisiana Shrimp and Crab Meat with Angel Hair Pasta

1/2 cup (1 stick) butter
1/2 cup extra-virgin olive oil
2 garlic cloves, minced
1 pound peeled uncooked
   medium shrimp
3/4 cup chopped green onions
1 1/2 cups half-and-half
3/4 cup (3 ounces) freshly grated
   Parmesan cheese

1 teaspoon cornstarch
1/4 cup water
1 pound crab meat
3/4 cup chopped fresh parsley
Salt and red pepper to taste
1 package fresh angel hair pasta,
   cooked

Melt the butter with the olive oil in a skillet. Add the garlic. Cook for about 30 seconds. Add the shrimp and sauté until the shrimp turn pink. Stir in the green onions, half-and-half and cheese. Cook for several minutes, stirring constantly. Dissolve the cornstarch in the water and stir into the shrimp mixture. Stir in the crab meat and parsley. Cook for 5 minutes or until heated through. Season with salt and red pepper. Pour over the hot pasta in a bowl and toss to coat. Serve immediately.

SERVES 6

Shrimp, Crab Meat and Eggplant Casserole

4 eggplant, peeled and cut into chunks
2 quarts boiling water
1/2 cup (1 stick) butter
3 onions, chopped
1 pound uncooked peeled
    medium shrimp
3/4 cup (or more) Italian-style
    bread crumbs

3/4 cup (3 ounces) (or more) grated
    Parmesan cheese
1 teaspoon Cajun or Creole seasoning
1 pound lump or claw crab meat
1/2 cup (1 stick) butter
5 slices day-old white or wheat bread,
    torn into bite-size pieces

Preheat the oven to 350 degrees. Cook the eggplant in the boiling water in a stockpot until tender; drain. Melt 1/2 cup butter in a large skillet. Add the onions. Sauté until light brown. Stir in the shrimp. Cook over medium heat for 10 to 15 minutes. Add the eggplant, bread crumbs, cheese and Cajun seasoning and mix well. Fold in the crab meat. Add more Parmesan cheese and bread crumbs to firm up the mixture if necessary. Spoon into a greased 9×13-inch baking dish. Bake for 45 minutes. Melt 1/2 cup butter in a skillet. Add the bread pieces. Sauté over medium heat until lightly browned. Sprinkle over the seafood mixture. Cook for 5 to 10 minutes longer or until the croutons are brown.

SERVES 10 TO 12

New Orleans–Style Barbecued Shrimp

4 pounds unpeeled headless shrimp,
    rinsed and drained
4 teaspoons pepper
2 teaspoons Worcestershire sauce

1/2 teaspoon garlic powder
1/2 teaspoon salt
2 cups (4 sticks) butter, melted

Place the shrimp in a heavy roasting pan or Dutch oven. Cook over medium to medium-high heat until the shrimp turn pink, stirring constantly. Remove from the heat. Sprinkle with the pepper, Worcestershire sauce, garlic powder and salt. Pour the butter over the shrimp. Bring to a boil over high heat. Reduce the heat to medium. Cook for 3 to 4 minutes, stirring occasionally. Adjust the heat as necessary to prevent the butter from burning. Remove from the heat. Let stand, covered, for as long as possible to allow the butter sauce to permeate the shrimp. Serve with toasted French bread.

SERVES 8

Boiled Shrimp C'est Bon!

Shrimp Boil
3 or 4 packets crab boil
1 to 2 pounds new potatoes

4 ears of fresh corn, shucked and halved
2 to 3 pounds unpeeled headless shrimp

Broccoli
1 or 2 bunches broccoli, cut into
    serving-size pieces

2 or 3 tablespoons margarine
Cajun or Creole seasoning to taste

Dipping Sauce
3/4 cup ketchup
1/4 cup mayonnaise (optional)
2 teaspoons Worcestershire sauce

1 teaspoon Cajun Power garlic sauce
    (optional)

For the shrimp boil, fill a large heavy-bottomed roasting pan or Dutch oven 2/3 full with water. Bring to a boil. Add the crab boil packets and potatoes. Cook until the potatoes are tender. Add the corn. Cook for 5 minutes or until tender. Add the shrimp. Cook for 5 to 6 minutes or until the shrimp turn pink. Drain the shrimp and vegetables.

For the broccoli, cook the broccoli in boiling water in a saucepan until tender; drain. Add the margarine and Cajun seasoning.

For the dipping sauce, combine the ketchup, mayonnaise, Worcestershire sauce and garlic sauce in a small bowl and mix well.

To assemble and serve, prepare individual portions of the dipping sauce for each person. Place the shrimp, potatoes and corn in a large serving bowl. Arrange the broccoli around the edge. Serve with French bread.

SERVES 6 TO 8

Shrimp Grillades

2 pounds deveined peeled shrimp
Cajun or Creole seasoning to taste
8 ounces sliced bacon
2 onions, chopped
1 cup chopped multi-colored bell peppers
1/2 cup (1 stick) butter
4 garlic cloves, minced

1/2 cup heavy cream
1/4 cup chopped fresh parsley
Salt and pepper to taste
Jalapeño Cheese Grits (page 138)
1/2 cup chopped green onions
1/2 cup chopped Roma tomatoes

Combine the shrimp and Cajun seasoning in a bowl. Cook the bacon in a large skillet over medium heat until crisp; drain, reserving the bacon drippings in the skillet. Crumble the bacon. Sauté the onions and bell peppers in the reserved bacon drippings over medium-high heat for 5 minutes or until tender. Add the butter and cook until melted, stirring constantly. Add the garlic and shrimp. Cook for 3 to 5 minutes or until the shrimp turn pink, stirring constantly. Stir in the cream. Cook for 5 minutes or until slightly thickened, stirring constantly. Add the parsley, salt and pepper. Remove from the heat. Serve over Jalapeño Cheese Grits. Top with the green onions, tomatoes and bacon.

SERVES 8

Lemon Shrimp Casserole

2 pounds cooked shrimp, peeled
2 cups cooked rice
2 cups (8 ounces) shredded sharp
    Cheddar cheese
1 (10-ounce) can cream of
    mushroom soup
1 green bell pepper, chopped

1/2 cup chopped onion
3 ribs celery, chopped
1/2 cup (1 stick) butter
1 teaspoon Cajun or Creole seasoning
    or to taste
4 to 6 lemons, thinly sliced

Preheat the oven to 375 degrees. Combine the shrimp, rice, cheese and mushroom soup in a large bowl and mix well. Sauté the bell pepper, onion and celery in the butter in a skillet until tender. Stir into the shrimp mixture. Add the Cajun seasoning. Pour into a buttered baking dish. Place the lemon slices over the top. Bake, covered with foil, for 25 to 30 minutes or until heated through.

SERVES 6 TO 8

"Big Pecan" Shrimp Jambalaya

1/2 cup (1 stick) margarine
1 cup chopped onion
1/2 cup chopped celery
1/4 cup chopped green bell pepper
1/2 cup fresh parsley, chopped
2 garlic cloves, minced
2 pounds peeled shrimp

1 (16-ounce) can tomato sauce
1 teaspoon salt
1/2 teaspoon black pepper
1/4 teaspoon cayenne pepper
3 cups water
1 1/2 cups uncooked rice
1/4 cup chopped green onion tops

Melt the margarine in a large skillet or saucepan. Add the onion, celery, bell pepper, parsley and garlic. Sauté until the onion is translucent. Stir in the shrimp, tomato sauce, salt, black pepper and cayenne pepper. Simmer for 15 minutes. Add the water and bring to a boil. Stir in the rice. Reduce the heat to low. Simmer, covered, for 20 minutes or until the liquid is absorbed. Sprinkle with the green onion tops.

SERVES 6

Pasta Jambalaya

1/2 cup Italian salad dressing
1/4 cup soy sauce
6 to 8 chicken thighs
2 links smoked sausage, chopped
1/4 cup olive oil
2 onions, chopped
3 ribs celery, chopped
1 green bell pepper, chopped

2 (10-ounce) cans chicken stock
1 garlic clove, crushed
1 teaspoon salt
1/8 teaspoon pepper
1 (12-ounce) package whole wheat
   spaghetti, broken into thirds
8 ounces fresh mushrooms, sliced

Combine the salad dressing and soy sauce in a shallow bowl. Add the chicken and turn to coat well. Marinate in the refrigerator for 2 to 3 hours. Brown the sausage in the olive oil in a skillet. Add the chicken thighs and sauté until brown. Add the onions, celery, bell pepper, chicken stock, garlic, salt and pepper and mix well. Bring to a boil. Add the spaghetti, fresh mushrooms and enough water to cover. Cook, covered, for 15 minutes. Serve immediately.

SERVES 6 TO 8

Jambalaya for a Crowd

8 chicken bouillon cubes

13 1/2 cups hot water

4 pounds smoked sausage, cut into
  3/4-inch slices

1 pound smoked pork tasso, cut into
  small pieces

Vegetable oil

4 pounds boneless skinless chicken
  breasts, cut into 2- to 3-inch cubes

3 pounds onions, chopped

3 green bell peppers, chopped

1 head garlic, chopped

3 tablespoons plus 2 teaspoons salt

3 1/2 teaspoons cayenne pepper

6 tablespoons Kitchen Bouquet

2 tablespoons Worcestershire sauce

8 cups uncooked long grain white rice

4 bunches green onions, chopped

1 bunch parsley, chopped

Dissolve the bouillon cubes in the water in a large saucepan. Cook the sausage and tasso in a small amount of oil in a 16-quart heavy pot until brown. Remove the sausage mixture and drain. Add the chicken to the drippings in the pot. Cook until golden brown. Remove the chicken and drain. Add the onions, bell peppers and garlic to the pot. Sauté until tender. Add the sausage mixture and chicken to the vegetables. Cook for 10 minutes. Stir in the bouillon, salt, cayenne pepper, Kitchen Bouquet and Worcestershire sauce. Bring to a boil. Reduce the heat to very low. Stir in the rice. Cook, covered, for 45 minutes or until the rice is tender. Stir in the green onions and parsley. Cook, covered, for 20 to 30 minutes longer.

SERVES 18

A Crowd Pleaser

Whether due to its blend of seasonings, its warm and filling nature, or its relatively inexpensive ingredients, jambalaya is a popular dish for serving a crowd. On game day, at festivals, or at large family gatherings, jambalaya often makes an appearance and can always be relied on to please the crowd. Gumbos served with steamed rice, seafood fettuccini, or tender-cooked roasts, prepared in quantity and served as sandwiches, are also South Louisiana crowd-satisfying favorites.

Coq au Vin

8 ounces pancetta or unsmoked bacon,
  cut into 1/2-inch pieces
1 frying chicken, cut up
Salt and pepper to taste
2 tablespoons butter or olive oil
2 carrots, sliced
2 onions, chopped
1 shallot, sliced
2 garlic cloves, chopped
2 tablespoons all-purpose flour
2 1/2 cups burgundy

1 1/2 tablespoons Cognac
8 ounces mushrooms, sliced
6 pearl onions
1 bay leaf
1 teaspoon thyme
1 teaspoon salt
1/4 teaspoon peppercorns, ground
2 tablespoons parsley
8 to 10 red potatoes, stripe peeled
  around the middle and cooked

Cook the pancetta in a cast-iron pot until brown. Remove the pancetta with a slotted spoon, leaving the drippings in the pot. Season the chicken with salt and pepper to taste. Sauté in the drippings until golden. Remove the chicken. Add the butter, carrots, onions, shallot and garlic to the pot. Cook until the vegetables are tender. Stir in the flour. Add the burgundy, Cognac, pancetta and chicken and stir well. Add the mushrooms, pearl onions, bay leaf, thyme, 1 teaspoon salt and peppercorns. Simmer, covered, over low heat for 1 hour. Remove and discard the bay leaf. Arrange the chicken on a platter. Pour the sauce over the chicken. Sprinkle with the parsley. Serve with the potatoes.

SERVES 6

Chicken Breasts with Green Peppercorns

6 large boneless skinless chicken breasts
2 1/2 tablespoons all-purpose flour
1 1/2 teaspoons (or more) salt
1 small onion, cut into wedges and
    separated
4 tablespoons butter

1/3 cup dry white wine or vermouth
1/2 cup half-and-half
1/2 teaspoon canned green peppercorns,
    rinsed and drained, or 1 teaspoon
    ground peppercorns

Place the chicken between 2 sheets of waxed paper and pound to 1/4-inch thickness. Mix the flour and salt in a shallow dish. Coat the chicken with the flour, shaking off the excess. Sauté 3 of the chicken breasts with 1/2 of the onion in 2 tablespoons of the butter in a skillet for 4 to 5 minutes on each side. Repeat with the remaining chicken breasts, onion and butter. Remove the chicken and onion to a serving dish. Let stand, covered, to keep warm. Add the wine, half-and-half and peppercorns to the skillet. Cook, scraping up the brown bits in the bottom of the skillet and crushing the peppercorns with the back of a spoon. Simmer for 3 to 4 minutes or until the sauce is smooth and slightly thickened. Spoon over the chicken.

SERVES 3 TO 6

Elegant Chicken

12 boneless skinless chicken breasts
3/4 cup (1 1/2 sticks) unsalted butter
2 teaspoons thyme
2 1/2 teaspoons salt
1 1/2 teaspoons cayenne pepper
1 1/2 teaspoons garlic powder

2 cups chopped onions
1/4 cup (1/2 stick) unsalted butter, melted
1 cup dry sherry
2 (8-ounce) cans sliced, button or chopped mushrooms, drained

Sauté the chicken breasts in 3/4 cup butter in a large skillet until brown on both sides. Combine the thyme, salt, cayenne pepper and garlic powder in a small bowl and mix well. Layer the chicken breasts in a Dutch oven, sprinkling the seasoning mixture and onions between the layers. Cook, covered, over low heat for 30 minutes. Rearrange the chicken breasts. Stir in the melted butter, sherry and mushrooms. Cook over low heat for 30 minutes or until the chicken is tender and the juices run clear. Adjust the seasonings to taste. Serve the chicken and sauce over crisp toast points.

SERVES 12

Creamy Italian Chicken

2 pounds boneless skinless chicken breasts, cut into strips
2 tablespoons olive oil
1/4 cup (1/2 stick) butter, melted
1/2 (8-ounce) tub cream cheese with chives

1 (10-ounce) can golden mushroom soup
1 envelope Italian salad dressing mix
1/2 cup (or more) white wine
Angel hair pasta, cooked

Sauté the chicken in the olive oil in a skillet until tender and cooked through. Combine the butter, cream cheese with chives, soup and salad dressing mix in a bowl and mix well. Pour over the chicken in the skillet. Stir in the wine. Cook over low heat until the sauce is smooth, adding more wine if needed for the desired consistency. Serve over angel hair pasta.

SERVES 4 TO 6

Southern Fried Chicken

2 cups all-purpose flour
1/2 teaspoon salt
1/4 teaspoon black pepper
1/4 teaspoon cayenne pepper (optional)
2 eggs

1/2 cup milk or buttermilk
4 or 5 boneless skinless chicken breasts,
   cut into 1/2×2-inch pieces
2 cups vegetable oil for frying
Salt and black pepper to taste

Combine the flour, 1/2 teaspoon salt, 1/4 teaspoon black pepper and cayenne pepper in a shallow dish. Whisk the eggs and milk together in a bowl. Coat the chicken with the flour mixture. Dip in the egg mixture and coat with the flour mixture again, shaking off the excess. Fry the chicken in a single layer in the hot oil in an 8- or 9-inch cast-iron skillet for 3 to 4 minutes on each side or until golden brown, turning once. Drain on paper towels. Season the warm chicken with salt and black pepper to taste.

SERVES 4 TO 6

Chili Lime Chicken Kabobs

3 tablespoons olive oil
1 1/2 tablespoons red wine vinegar
3 tablespoons frozen limeade
   concentrate
1 teaspoon chili powder
1/2 teaspoon onion powder
1/2 teaspoon garlic powder

1/2 teaspoon paprika
1 teaspoon chipolte pepper sauce
Pinch of salt
Pinch of freshly ground pepper
1 pound chicken tenders
Lime wedges (optional)

Combine the olive oil, vinegar and limeade concentrate in a large bowl and mix well. Whisk in the chili powder, onion powder, garlic powder, paprika, chipolte pepper sauce, salt and pepper. Add the chicken tenders. Marinate, covered, in the refrigerator for 8 to 10 hours. Preheat the grill. Thread the chicken onto skewers and place on a grill rack. Grill over medium-high coals for 10 minutes or until the juices run clear. Place a lime wedge on the end of each skewer before serving.

MAKES 10 TO 12 KABOBS

Creamy Chicken Lasagna

1 chicken bouillon cube
1/4 cup hot water
3 boneless skinless chicken breasts,
    cooked and shredded
8 ounces cream cheese, softened
1 cup (4 ounces) shredded
    mozzarella cheese
1 (10-ounce) package frozen chopped
    spinach, thawed and drained

1 (14-ounce) can artichoke hearts,
    drained and diced
Seasonings to taste
1 (26-ounce) jar tomato and basil
    spaghetti sauce
6 uncooked lasagna noodles
1 cup (4 ounces) shredded
    mozzarella cheese

Preheat the oven to 350 degrees. Dissolve the bouillon cube in the hot water in a large bowl. Add the chicken, cream cheese, 1 cup mozzarella cheese, spinach and artichokes and mix well. Add seasonings to taste. Layer 1/3 of the spaghetti sauce, 1/2 of the chicken mixture and 3 of the lasagna noodles in a 9×9-inch baking dish. Continue layering with 1/2 of the remaining spaghetti sauce, the remaining chicken mixture, the remaining 3 noodles and the remaining spaghetti sauce. Top with 1 cup mozzarella cheese. Bake for 45 minutes.

SERVES 6

Parmesan Chicken

6 boneless skinless chicken breasts
1/2 teaspoon salt
1/2 teaspoon Cajun or Creole seasoning
1/2 teaspoon garlic powder
1/2 cup (1 stick) butter or margarine

1 teaspoon Worcestershire sauce
Juice of 1 lemon
1 cup baking mix
1/2 cup (2 ounces) grated
    Parmesan cheese

Preheat the oven to 350 degrees. Season the chicken with the salt, Cajun seasoning and garlic powder. Melt the butter with the Worcestershire sauce and lemon juice in a small saucepan. Mix the baking mix and cheese in a shallow dish. Dip the chicken in the butter mixture and coat with the baking mix. Place the chicken in a single layer in a lightly greased 9×13-inch baking dish. Pour the remaining butter mixture over the chicken. Bake, uncovered, for 1 hour or until the chicken is cooked through.

SERVES 4 TO 6

Chicken with Tomatoes and Green Chiles over Vermicelli

2 chicken breasts
Pinch of salt
1 onion, chopped
1 green bell pepper, chopped
1/4 cup (1/2 stick) butter
1 (10-ounce) can cream of
　mushroom soup

1 (10-ounce) can tomatoes with
　green chiles
1 small can peas, drained
1 small can mushrooms, drained
1 pound Velveeta cheese, shredded
7 ounces vermicelli, cooked and drained

Preheat the oven to 350 degrees. Cook the chicken in boiling salted water in a saucepan until tender and cooked through. Drain the chicken and cool slightly. Shred the chicken. Sauté the onion and bell pepper in the butter in a large skillet until tender. Stir in the chicken, soup, tomatoes with green chiles, peas, mushrooms and cheese. Cook until the cheese is melted, stirring constantly. Stir in the vermicelli. Pour into a greased 9×13-inch baking dish. Bake for 30 to 35 minutes or until bubbly. Serve with green beans and a salad.

SERVES 4 TO 6

Chicken and Wild Rice Casserole

6 chicken quarters
Salt and pepper to taste
Chopped onion to taste
1 package wild rice mix
2 (4-ounce) cans mushrooms
2/3 cup chopped onion

3/4 cup (1 1/2 sticks) butter
1/2 cup all-purpose flour
2 cups chicken broth
2 cups heavy cream
1/2 cup slivered almonds (optional)

Cook the chicken in boiling salted water with a little pepper and chopped onion to taste in a large soup pot until tender. Chop the chicken, discarding the skin and bones. Cook the wild rice using the package directions. Drain the mushrooms, reserving the liquid. Preheat the oven to 350 degrees. Sauté 2/3 cup chopped onion in the butter in a skillet until tender. Stir in the flour. Add the chicken broth, reserved mushroom liquid, cream, salt and pepper. Cook until smooth and thickened, stirring constantly. Combine the chicken, wild rice and mushrooms in a large bowl. Add the sauce and mix well. Pour into a greased 3-quart baking dish. Top with the almonds. Bake for 30 minutes or until bubbly.

Note: You may also bake in 2 small greased baking dishes.

SERVES 6

Thyme Balsamic Chicken

4 boneless skinless chicken breasts
1 tablespoon olive oil
2 garlic cloves, cut into halves
    lengthwise
1/2 cup chicken broth
1/2 cup balsamic vinegar

1 tablespoon chopped fresh thyme,
    or 1 teaspoon dried thyme
1 teaspoon kosher salt
Freshly ground pepper to taste
1 tablespoon unsalted butter

Pound the chicken into uniform thickness between 2 sheets of waxed paper. Heat the olive oil and garlic in a skillet over medium-high heat until the garlic begins to brown. Add the chicken. Cook for 4 minutes or until golden on both sides. Add the chicken broth, vinegar, thyme, kosher salt and pepper. Simmer, covered, over medium-low heat for 4 minutes. Remove the chicken to a serving platter and cover with foil. Cook the sauce over high heat for 4 minutes longer. Whisk in the butter. Pour over the chicken.

SERVES 4

Tomato Chicken

6 chicken breasts with skin and bones,
    or 1 frying chicken, cut up
Cajun or Creole seasoning
Vegetable oil

2 (28-ounce) cans whole tomatoes
2 onions, chopped
5 garlic cloves, minced
Olive oil

Preheat the oven to 375 degrees. Sprinkle the chicken generously with Cajun seasoning. Sauté in a little vegetable oil in a large skillet until golden brown on both sides (the chicken will be only partially cooked); drain. Drain the tomatoes, reserving the juice. Purée the whole tomatoes in a food processor. Combine the onions, garlic and a small amount of olive oil in a large microwave-safe bowl. Microwave on High for 10 minutes, stirring occasionally. Add the puréed tomatoes and the reserved tomato juice. Microwave on High for 15 minutes. Place the chicken in a large 9×13-inch baking dish. Pour the tomato sauce over the chicken. Bake for 1 1/2 hours. Serve with your favorite pasta.

SERVES 6

Cajun Fried Turkey

Injectable Marinade

1 cup water
3/4 cup garlic juice
3/4 cup onion juice
1/3 cup hot red pepper sauce
1/4 cup Cajun or Creole seasoning

1/4 cup jalapeño chile juice
  (for poultry marinade only)
2 tablespoons Creole mustard
1 tablespoon Worcestershire sauce

Deep-Fried Turkey

1 (14-pound) turkey, thawed
Creole mustard

Cajun or Creole seasoning
5 gallons peanut oil

For the marinade, combine the water, garlic juice, onion juice, hot red pepper sauce, Cajun seasoning, jalapeño chile juice, Creole mustard and Worcestershire sauce in a blender and process until smooth. Pour into a jar. Chill for at least 2 days before use.

For the turkey, pour 1 cup of the marinade into a tall glass, reserving the remaining marinade for future use. Fill a meat injector with the marinade. Inject the marinade deep into the turkey muscle, inserting the needle at 2-inch intervals. Rub the turkey with Creole mustard and sprinkle generously with Cajun seasoning. Heat the peanut oil in a heavy 30-quart aluminum or stainless steel frying pot over a butane burner to 350 degrees. Add the turkey. Fry for 4 minutes per pound or until the juices run clear. Extract the turkey from the oil. Let stand for 10 minutes before slicing.

SERVES 15

The New Tradition

Louisiana's holidays have taken on a new twist in recent years with the increasing popularity of Fried Turkey. To safely fry a turkey for your event, you must first purchase a turkey frying kit. Due to the large amount of hot oil used, strict adherence to all safety and preparation instructions enclosed with the kit is essential. For a flavorful bird, use a meat injector—available through mail order as well as at most kitchen supply stores. Ensure uniform flavor by evenly injecting your chosen marinade throughout the bird.

Meat & Game

Grilled Beef Tenderloin with Mushroom Wine Sauce

Beef

2 pounds beef tenderloin

3 tablespoons olive oil

1 1/2 teaspoons salt

1 1/2 teaspoons pepper

Mushroom Wine Sauce

3/4 cup (1 1/2 sticks) butter or margarine

6 shallots, chopped

4 green onions, chopped

2 garlic cloves, minced

4 ounces sliced mushrooms

2 tablespoons all-purpose flour

1 (10-ounce) can beef consommé

3/4 cup red wine

For the beef, preheat the grill. Coat the beef with the olive oil. Rub a mixture of the salt and pepper into the beef. Place on a grill rack. Grill over hot coals for 30 minutes for medium or to the desired degree of doneness.

For the sauce, melt the butter in a skillet over medium-high heat. Add the shallots, green onions and garlic. Sauté for 2 to 5 minutes. Add the mushrooms. Sauté for 5 to 8 minutes. Stir in the flour. Cook for 1 to 2 minutes, stirring constantly. Stir in the beef consommé and red wine. Cook for 5 to 8 minutes or until the sauce has thickened. Serve immediately over the beef.

SERVES 6 TO 8

Beef Brisket "To Die For"

1 (8- to 10-pound) brisket, trimmed
Cajun or Creole seasoning
1³/4 cups ketchup
1 cup packed brown sugar
1 (10-ounce) can tomato soup
2 tablespoons liquid smoke

2 tablespoons yellow mustard or
  Dijon mustard
2 tablespoons Worcestershire Sauce
1/2 cup sour cream
1 teaspoon prepared horseradish

Preheat the oven to 325 to 350 degrees. Season the brisket generously with Cajun seasoning in a large roasting pan with cover. Combine the ketchup, brown sugar, soup, liquid smoke, yellow mustard and Worcestershire Sauce in a bowl and mix well. Pour over the brisket. Bake, covered, for 3 to 4 hours or until fork-tender. Skim the fat from the roasting pan drippings. Measure 1 cup of the drippings and combine with the sour cream and horseradish in a bowl. Serve with the brisket.

SERVES 8 TO 10

Dripped Beef

1 (4-pound) boneless chuck roast
Tabasco sauce to taste
Worcestershire sauce to taste
Garlic powder to taste
Salt and pepper to taste

2 onions, chopped
6 ribs celery, chopped
1 green bell pepper, chopped
1 bottle Bovril beef extract

Preheat the oven to 350 degrees. Season the beef with Tabasco sauce, Worcestershire sauce, garlic powder, salt and pepper. (Salt lightly as the beef extract is very salty.) Place the beef in a large roasting pan with cover. Add the onions, celery, bell pepper and beef extract. Fill the empty Bovril bottle with water and pour over the roast. Bake, covered, for 5 hours. Slice the beef and add to the gravy. Serve on small buns or potato rolls, or over rice.

SERVES 10 TO 12

Favorite Sandwiches

Serve Dripped Beef at your next holiday open house or cocktail party and you will have a request or two for the recipe. Place the slow-cooked, tender roast alongside a tray or a basket of petite potato rolls so that guests can make sandwiches. Small bowls of stone-ground mustard, horseradish spread, and mayonnaise will complete the offering.

Meat Pies

2 cups all-purpose flour
1 cup (2 sticks) butter, softened
8 ounces cream cheese, softened
1 1/2 teaspoons salt
1 teaspoon red pepper
1 onion, finely chopped

1 rib celery, finely chopped
1 pound ground beef
1 garlic clove, chopped
1 (10-ounce) can cream of
  mushroom soup

Combine the flour, butter, cream cheese, 1/2 teaspoon of the salt and 1/4 teaspoon of the red pepper in a mixing bowl and beat until well combined. Chill the pastry, covered, for 20 minutes. Sauté the onion and celery in a small nonstick skillet until the onion is translucent. Brown the ground beef in a skillet, stirring until the ground beef is crumbly; drain. Stir in the sautéed vegetables, garlic, soup, remaining salt and red pepper. Cook for 5 minutes. Adjust the seasonings. Preheat the oven to 350 degrees. Shape the pastry into small balls. Roll the balls as thin as possible on a lightly floured surface. Cut out circles with a biscuit cutter. Place 1 teaspoon of the meat filling on 1/2 of the dough circle. Fold the dough over the filling and press the edges with a fork to seal. Place on a baking sheet. Bake for 10 to 12 minutes or until golden brown.

MAKES 20 TO 25 PIES

Sunday Roast

1/4 cup vegetable oil
1 large eye-of-round roast
Cajun or Creole seasoning

3 (10-ounce) cans beef broth
3/4 cup prepared dry roux
2 (4-ounce) cans sliced mushrooms

Preheat the oven to 350 degrees. Pour the oil into a large roasting pan with cover. Sprinkle all sides of the roast with Cajun seasoning. Place the roast in the pan. Bake, covered, for 1 hour. Pour 1 can of the beef broth over the roast. Bake for 1 hour. Remove the roast to a cutting board. Mix the 2 remaining cans beef broth and the dry roux in a large bowl. Pour into the pan drippings. Bring to a boil, stirring constantly. Stir in the mushrooms. Slice the roast and serve with the gravy.

SERVES 8

No Oil?

Dry roux, made at home or store-bought, has become popular as free time becomes less abundant and waistlines become more so. Dry roux is perfect as a thickener or to add a richer taste to numerous dishes. To prepare, heat a large cast-iron skillet over medium heat. Add 1 cup of flour and cook for 15 to 25 minutes or until the flour is a medium brown, stirring constantly. Cool and store for future use.

Fried Kibbies

Hoshua (Meat Stuffing)
2 pounds ground chuck
1/4 cup (1/2 stick) butter
1 tablespoon salt
1 teaspoon red pepper
1/4 teaspoon black pepper

1/4 teaspoon cinnamon
1/4 teaspoon allspice
4 pounds onions, chopped, or 3 pounds
   frozen chopped onions, thawed
1/3 to 1/2 cup pine nuts, roasted

Kibbi Nayeh (Raw Kibbi)
2 cups (1 pound) cracked wheat
   (bulgur #1, fine)
2 cups (1 pound) cracked wheat
   (bulgur #2, medium)
1 teaspoon salt
1/2 teaspoon red pepper
1/8 teaspoon each cinnamon and allspice

2 pounds very lean beef (top round or
   top sirloin), ground 4 times
3 1/2 teaspoons salt
1/2 teaspoon red pepper
2 tablespoons dried mint, crushed
Ice water
Vegetable oil for deep-frying

For the meat stuffing, brown the ground chuck in the butter in a skillet, stirring until crumbly. Stir in the next 5 ingredients. Add the onions. Cook, covered, over medium-high heat for 30 minutes, stirring frequently. Stir in the pine nuts. Reduce the heat to low. Cook, uncovered, for 20 minutes or until the onions are translucent; drain. Adjust the seasonings. Chill, covered, for 8 to 10 hours.

For the kibbi, mix the fine and medium cracked wheat in a large mixing bowl. Rinse with cold water and pour off the excess water. Rinse again and pour off the excess water. Add 1 teaspoon salt, 1/2 teaspoon red pepper, cinnamon and allspice and mix well. Let stand for 1 hour or until the wheat is soft and the water is absorbed. Add the ground beef to the wheat and knead well. Season with 3 1/2 teaspoons salt, 1/2 teaspoon red pepper and mint. Add small amounts of ice water gradually until the mixture is firm enough to roll into balls, stirring constantly. Adjust the seasonings.

Roll the kibbi mixture by 1/2 cupfuls into golf-ball size balls, using hands dipped in ice water to prevent sticking. Hollow each ball to form a 1/8-inch shell. Place a heaping teaspoon of the meat stuffing in each shell. Seal the shell over the stuffing and press gently to form a football shape. Place the kibbies on a baking sheet lined with waxed paper. Freeze for 8 to 10 hours. Deep-fry the kibbies in hot oil in a deep fryer for 6 to 7 minutes or until golden brown.

MAKES ABOUT 50

Planning Ahead

Whether making kibbies for the first or fiftieth time, you'll find the preparation much easier with a little simple planning. Locate a butcher familiar with the preparation of kibbi meat to ensure it is appropriately trimmed and ground the necessary four times. Then arrange your schedule to allow the meat stuffing to be cooked and refrigerated overnight. The next morning, the kibbi shells can be filled with the cooled stuffing. The completed kibbies may be fried immediately or frozen for future use.

Veal and Tomato Ragout with Potatoes, Cinnamon and Cream

2 pounds boneless veal stew meat,
　cut into 1-inch pieces
Salt and pepper to taste
1/4 cup all-purpose flour
3 tablespoons butter
1 tablespoon olive oil
2 onions, chopped
2 ribs celery, chopped

1 1/4 cups vermouth
2 cups tomato sauce
1 cup (or more) water
3 tablespoons fresh parsley, chopped
2 cinnamon sticks
1 1/4 pounds white potatoes, peeled and
　cut into 1/2-inch slices
1/2 cup heavy cream

Season the veal with salt and pepper to taste. Place the flour in a paper bag. Add the veal pieces and shake well. Melt the butter with the olive oil in a heavy pan. Add the veal in batches. Cook for 6 minutes per batch or until browned on all sides. Remove the veal to a bowl. Add the onions and celery to the pan. Sauté for 5 minutes or until the onions are tender. Add the veal and vermouth to the pan. Bring to a boil. Boil for 3 minutes or until the liquid is reduced by half. Stir in the tomato sauce, water, parsley and cinnamon sticks. Bring to a boil. Reduce the heat to low. Simmer, covered, for 1 1/4 hours, stirring occasionally. Add the potatoes, cream and salt and pepper to taste. Simmer for 1 hour or until the veal and potatoes are very tender, stirring frequently and thinning with water if necessary. Remove and discard the cinnamon sticks.

Note: You may use beef stew meat instead of veal stew meat.

SERVES 6

Lamb Chops Persillade

Lamb Chops

1/4 cup Dijon mustard

1/2 teaspoon soy sauce

1 teaspoon olive oil

6 (1 1/4-inch-thick) lamb chops

Olive oil

Persillade Coating

1/3 cup minced fresh flat-leaf parsley

1/3 cup dry bread crumbs

1/4 to 1/2 teaspoon salt

1/4 to 1/2 teaspoon pepper

2 small garlic cloves, crushed

Minced fresh thyme to taste

1 tablespoon olive oil

For the lamb chops, combine the Dijon mustard, soy sauce and 1 teaspoon olive oil in a bowl and mix well. Place the lamb chops in a shallow dish. Brush the chops with 1/2 of the mustard mixture. Marinate in the refrigerator for 1 to 2 hours. Preheat the oven to 400 degrees. Coat a large skillet with olive oil. Sear the chops in the skillet over high heat until browned on both sides. Transfer to a baking pan. Bake for 20 minutes. Remove the chops from the oven. Brush with the remaining mustard mixture.

For the persillade coating, combine the parsley, bread crumbs, salt, pepper, garlic, thyme and olive oil in a small bowl and mix well. Coat the chops with the persillade, pressing firmly with the back of a spoon. Bake for 10 to 15 minutes longer or until the chops are to the desired degree of doneness and the coating is crisp.

SERVES 6

Lamb or Beef Kabobs

Barbecue Sauce
1 cup ketchup
1/2 cup water
1/4 cup sugar
1/4 cup steak sauce

1/4 cup cider vinegar
1/4 cup Worcestershire sauce
1 tablespoon vegetable oil
2 teaspoons salt

Kabobs
1 1/2 pounds lamb or beef, cut into
  1-inch cubes
2 tomatoes, cut into wedges

2 green bell peppers, cut into chunks
2 onions, coarsely chopped

For the barbecue sauce, combine the ketchup, water, sugar, steak sauce, cider vinegar, Worcestershire sauce, oil and salt in a saucepan. Bring to a boil, stirring constantly. Adjust the seasonings. Let cool.

For the kabobs, place the lamb in a shallow dish. Pour 1/2 of the barbecue sauce over the lamb. Marinate in the refrigerator for 8 to 10 hours. Drain the lamb, reserving the marinade. Thread the lamb cubes alternately with the tomatoes, bell peppers and onions alternately onto skewers. Place on a grill rack. Grill over hot coals to desired degree of doneness, basting frequently with the reserved marinade. Reheat the remaining barbecue sauce and serve with the kabobs.

SERVES 4

Pork Tenderloin with Bourbon Marinade

1 (2- to 3-pound) pork tenderloin
1/2 cup soy sauce
1/2 cup bourbon

6 scallions, chopped
3/4 cup sour cream
2 tablespoons prepared horseradish

Place the pork tenderloin in a shallow baking dish. Combine the soy sauce, bourbon and scallions in a small bowl and mix well. Pour over the pork. Marinate in the refrigerator for 6 to 8 hours, turning the pork after 3 to 4 hours. Preheat the oven to 350 degrees. Bake the pork for 30 to 40 minutes or until cooked through. Slice into 1/2-inch medallions. Combine the sour cream and horseradish in a small bowl and mix well. Serve with the pork.

SERVES 6 TO 8

Injected Pork Roast with Tangy Satsuma Sauce

Pork Roast
1 (3- to 4-pound) boneless pork loin,
center rib or end roast,
tied with string
1 cup Injectable Marinade (page 161)
1 teaspoon crushed marjoram leaves, or
1/2 teaspoon ground marjoram

1 teaspoon dry mustard
1 teaspoon Cajun or Creole seasoning
2 teaspoons finely shredded satsuma
orange zest
1/2 cup satsuma orange juice
1/4 cup packed brown sugar

Tangy Satsuma Sauce
Drippings from pork roast
1 envelope brown gravy mix

3/4 cup water
4 satsuma oranges, peeled and sectioned

For the roast, preheat the oven to 325 degrees. Place the roast in a Dutch oven. Fill a meat injector with the marinade. Inject the marinade deep into the pork muscle, inserting the needle at 2-inch intervals until all the marinade has been used. Rub the roast with a mixture of the marjoram, dry mustard and Cajun seasoning. Bake, uncovered, for 1 1/2 hours. Combine the orange zest, orange juice and brown sugar in a small bowl and mix well. Spoon over the roast. Roast for 30 minutes or to 155 degrees on a meat thermometer, basting with the pan juices every 10 minutes. Transfer the roast to a serving platter. Let stand for 10 minutes before slicing.

For the satsuma sauce, place the Dutch oven with the drippings over medium heat. Dissolve the gravy mix in the water in a small bowl. Stir into the drippings, scraping up the browned bits on the bottom of the pan. Cook until thick and bubbly, stirring constantly. Adjust the seasonings. Stir in the satsuma sections. Cook until heated through. Serve the sauce ladled over the sliced pork.

SERVES 8 TO 10

So Sweet, So Good

A type of mandarin, satsumas are abundant in the early days of South Louisiana's winter and are commonly shared between generous gardeners and their eager neighbors. Due to their smallish size, sweet pulp, and easily "zippable" skins, satsumas are a popular lunch box treat. They also brighten a spinach salad or serve as a creative ingredient in favorite recipes—perhaps in a glaze for duck, a citrus-based cocktail, or a zesty satsuma marinade.

Pork Loin Roast with Hoppin' John Stuffing

1 onion, chopped
1/2 green bell pepper, chopped
2 tablespoons olive oil
11/2 cups cooked long grain rice
1 (15-ounce) can black-eyed peas,
    drained and rinsed
1/2 cup diced cooked country ham

1/2 teaspoon sugar
1/2 teaspoon salt
1/4 teaspoon Tabasco sauce, or to taste
1 egg, lightly beaten
1 (2- to 3-pound) boneless
    pork loin roast

Preheat the oven to 375 degrees. Sauté the onion and bell pepper in the olive oil in a skillet over medium-high heat for 5 to 7 minutes or until tender. Add the rice, black-eyed peas, ham, sugar, salt and Tabasco sauce and mix well. Stir in the egg. Remove from the heat and set aside. Make a lengthwise cut down the center of the pork loin, cutting to within 1/2 inch of the bottom. Make a horizontal cut from the bottom of the first cut to within 1/2 inch of the left side. Repeat the cut on the right side. Open the roast and place between 2 sheets of heavy-duty plastic wrap. Pound the roast into a 1/2-inch thickness, using a meat mallet or rolling pin. Spoon 11/2 cups of the stuffing evenly over the roast, leaving a 1/2-inch margin. Roll up to enclose the filling. Tie with string at 1-inch intervals. Place the roast seam side down in a lightly greased 7×11-inch baking dish. Bake for 55 to 60 minutes or until cooked through. Reheat the remaining stuffing and serve with the roast.

SERVES 6 TO 8

New Year's Luck

More than one or two South Louisiana families are steadfast in their respect for the old adage that black-eyed peas served on New Year's Day bring a year of good fortune. Pork Loin Roast with Hoppin' John Stuffing is a perfect choice for your New Year's Day gathering. Its use of black-eyed peas is a crowd-pleasing way to ensure that you and your guests have good luck in the days to come.

Stuffed Pork Chops

1 onion, finely chopped
3/4 cup finely chopped multi-colored
    bell peppers
2 ribs celery, finely chopped
2 garlic cloves, minced
3 tablespoons butter or olive oil
1/3 cup chopped fresh mushrooms
1/2 cup toasted bread crumbs
2 tablespoons chopped fresh parsley
1 teaspoon salt

1/4 teaspoon black pepper
1/4 teaspoon red pepper
Pinch of dried thyme
1 egg, lightly beaten
4 (11/4-inch-thick) pork chops
    with pockets
Cajun or Creole seasoning to taste
2 tablespoons vegetable oil or nonstick
    cooking spray

Preheat the oven to 375 degrees. Sauté the onion, bell peppers, celery and garlic in the butter in a skillet over medium heat until the vegetables are tender. Stir in the mushrooms, bread crumbs, parsley, salt, black pepper, red pepper and thyme. Remove from the heat. Stir in the egg. Season the pork chops with Cajun seasoning. Spoon the filling into the pork chop pockets. Sauté the chops in the oil in a skillet until golden brown on both sides. Remove the chops to an 8×12-inch baking dish coated with nonstick cooking spray. Bake, covered, for 1 hour, adding a little water as necessary to prevent burning. Remove the cover. Bake for 20 minutes longer.

SERVES 4

Red Beans and Sausage

2 pounds hot hickory-smoked
   sausage, sliced
1 red bell pepper, finely chopped
1 green bell pepper, finely chopped
3 ribs celery, finely chopped
1 small onion, finely chopped
   (about 1 cup chopped onion)
4 garlic cloves, minced

3 (15-ounce) cans New Orleans-style
   red kidney beans, drained
1 (15-ounce) can tomato sauce
1 (15-ounce) can water
3 tablespoons Pickapeppa sauce
1 tablespoon Worcestershire sauce
2 teaspoons Tabasco sauce

Brown the sausage in a Dutch oven. Remove the sausage. Add the bell peppers, celery, onion and garlic to the drippings. Sauté until the vegetables are tender. Stir in the kidney beans, tomato sauce, water, Pickapeppa sauce, Worcestershire sauce and Tabasco sauce. Simmer for 15 minutes. Stir in the sausage. Simmer, covered, for 1 1/2 hours. Serve over rice.

SERVES 6

Stuffed Duck Breast

8 duck breasts
4 cups milk or buttermilk
3 ounces cream cheese, softened.
1 small jar sliced jalapeño chiles

1 pound sliced bacon
Salt and pepper to taste
1 cup (or more) cane syrup

Combine the duck breasts and the milk in a shallow dish. Marinate in the refrigerator for 8 to 10 hours. Preheat the oven to 350 degrees. Mix the cream cheese and jalapeño chiles in a bowl. Slit a pocket in each duck breast. Spoon the cream cheese mixture into the pockets. Wrap the bacon slices around each breast, covering completely. Secure with wooden picks. Place the breasts in a roasting pan. Season with salt and pepper. Pour the cane syrup over the breasts. Bake for 30 to 40 minutes or until cooked through, basting frequently.

SERVES 8

Duck Weight

South Louisiana hunters may return from the duck blind with several types of duck, making it necessary to consider weight in making recipe adjustments and substitutions. The smallish and commonplace teal often weigh no more than one-half pound. Mallards easily double that size, weighing up to two pounds. Domestic-raised ducks, available at your market or specialty food store, are considerably weightier, often ranging up to six pounds.

Wild Goose with Currant Sauce

1 tablespoon all-purpose flour
1 each apple and orange,
   cut into quarters
6 pitted dried plums, chopped (optional)
1 (3- to 4-pound) goose
1 envelope onion soup mix

1 cup each red wine and water
1/4 cup red currant jelly
1/4 cup ketchup
1/4 cup port
1/4 cup Worcestershire sauce
2 tablespoons butter

Shake the flour in a large cooking bag. Place the apple quarters, orange quarters and dried plums in the goose cavity. Place the goose in the cooking bag in a large shallow baking dish. Combine the soup mix, wine and water in a bowl and mix well. Pour into the bag and seal. Marinate in the refrigerator for 4 to 12 hours. Preheat the oven to 350 degrees. Turn the goose breast side up. Cut 5 or 6 slits in the bag to allow the steam to escape. Bake for 2 1/2 to 3 hours or until cooked through. Combine the jelly, ketchup, port, Worcestershire sauce and butter in a small saucepan. Cook over medium heat until heated through. Remove the goose from the cooking bag, reserving the gravy. Cut each breast into thin slices. Serve the goose and gravy with the currant sauce on the side or add the sliced goose to the currant sauce. Serve with wild rice and/or sweet potatoes.

SERVES 4

Smothered Doves

8 doves
Salt, black pepper and red pepper to taste
1 onion, minced
1 rib celery, minced
1/2 green bell pepper, minced
2 garlic cloves, minced
6 slices bacon, chopped

1/2 cup peanut oil or other vegetable oil
2 tablespoons peanut oil or other
   vegetable oil
2 tablespoons all-purpose flour
1 small onion, chopped
1 cup water
1 (4-ounce) can sliced mushrooms

Preheat the oven to 350 degrees. Season the doves with salt, black pepper and red pepper. Mix the minced onion, celery, bell pepper, garlic and bacon in a bowl. Spoon 1 teaspoon of the vegetable mixture into each of the dove cavities. Brown the doves in 1/2 cup peanut oil in an oven-proof skillet or Dutch oven. Remove the doves from the skillet. Strain the oil, discarding the oil and reserving the browned particles. Add 2 tablespoons peanut oil to the skillet. Stir in the flour. Cook until caramel color, stirring constantly. Add the chopped onion. Cook until the onion is tender. Add the water. Cook until thickened, stirring constantly and adding more water if needed to make a gravy consistency. Place the doves breast side down in the gravy. Add the reserved browned particles. Bake, covered, for 1 hour. Stir in the remaining vegetable mixture. Simmer until the doves are tender. Add the mushrooms. Adjust the seasonings. Serve the doves and gravy over rice.

SERVES 4

Grilled Venison Backstrap

1 venison backstrap   *4 garlic cloves*
1 bottle Allegro marinade   *4 slices bacon*

Combine the venison and the marinade in a large shallow dish. Marinate in the refrigerator for 24 hours. Preheat the grill. Cut 4 slits in the backstrap and insert the garlic cloves. Wrap the bacon slices around the backstrap and secure with wooden picks. Place on a grill rack. Sear over hot coals on all sides. Reduce the heat to medium-low. Grill for 15 minutes for rare or 30 minutes for well done or to the desired degree of doneness, turning occasionally. Slice and serve.

SERVES 6 TO 8

A Decision to Make

Venison Backstrap Marinade is an excellent alternative preparation for backstrap. Combine 3/4 cup soy sauce, 3/4 cup olive oil, 1/2 cup Tabasco Caribbean steak sauce and 1/2 teaspoon pepper in a sealable plastic bag and mix well. Add 10-inch backstrap sections and seal the bag well. Marinate in the refrigerator for 5 to 12 hours, shaking the bag every few hours. Grill the venison over hot coals for 5 minutes on each side for medium or to desired degree of doneness.

Mushroom Venison Roast

1 (3- to 4-pound) venison roast
Salt and pepper to taste
2 garlic cloves, minced
Vegetable oil
2 cups sliced mushrooms

1 1/2 cups chopped onions
2 (10-ounce) cans French onion soup
1 (10-ounce) can cream of
   mushroom soup

Season the roast with salt and pepper. Cut slits in the roast and insert the garlic. Brown the roast in a little oil in a Dutch oven. Stir in the mushrooms, onions, onion soup and mushroom soup. Cook, covered, over low heat for 1 to 2 hours or until the roast is tender, stirring frequently.

SERVES 6 TO 8

Venison Meatballs

1 pound ground venison
3 tablespoons grated Parmesan cheese
2 tablespoons garlic powder
2 tablespoons minced onion

1 teaspoon parsley flakes
1 egg, beaten
Salt and pepper to taste
1/2 cup fine dry seasoned bread crumbs

Preheat the oven to 350 degrees. Combine the venison, cheese, garlic powder, onion, parsley flakes, egg, salt and pepper in a large bowl and mix gently using your hands. Stir in the bread crumbs. Shape into 1-inch balls and place on a greased baking sheet. Bake for 10 to 12 minutes or until cooked through. Stir the meatballs into your favorite tomato sauce and serve over hot pasta.

Note: You may fry the meatballs in hot oil in a skillet instead of baking.

SERVES 4 TO 6

Desserts & Sweets

Red Delicious Apple Cake

3 cups all-purpose flour
2 teaspoons ground cinnamon
1 1/2 teaspoons baking soda
1 teaspoon salt
1 1/4 cups vegetable oil
2 cups sugar

2 eggs
2 teaspoons vanilla extract
1/2 cup milk
3 cups finely chopped, peeled Red
    Delicious apples
1 cup walnuts, chopped

Preheat the oven to 350 degrees. Sift the flour, cinnamon, baking soda and salt together. Combine the oil and sugar in a mixing bowl and mix well. Add the eggs 1 at a time, mixing well after each addition. Beat in the vanilla. Add the flour mixture alternately with the milk, mixing well after each addition. Do not overbeat. Stir in the apples and walnuts. Pour into a greased and floured bundt pan. Bake for 1 hour or until the cake tests done. Cool in the pan for 20 minutes. Invert onto a serving plate.

SERVES 10 TO 12

Banana Cake with Caramel Icing

Cake
1 (2-layer) package yellow cake mix
2 ripe bananas, mashed (about 1 cup)
1 cup water
1/2 cup vegetable oil
1/2 cup packed light brown sugar

3 eggs
1 teaspoon ground cinnamon
2 teaspoons crème de banane liqueur
  (optional)

Caramel Icing
1/2 cup (1 stick) butter
1/2 cup packed light brown sugar
1/2 cup packed dark brown sugar

1/4 cup milk or evaporated milk
2 cups confectioners' sugar, sifted
1 teaspoon vanilla extract

Assembly
1 cup chopped pecans, toasted

For the cake, preheat the oven to 350 degrees. Combine the cake mix, bananas, water, oil, brown sugar, eggs, cinnamon and crème de banane liqueur in a mixing bowl and beat until smooth and creamy. Pour into 2 greased and floured 9-inch round cake pans. Bake for 30 to 35 minutes or until the tops are brown and a wooden pick inserted in the center of each layer comes out clean. Cool in the pans for 10 minutes. Remove to wire racks to cool completely.

For the icing, combine the butter, light brown sugar and dark brown sugar in a heavy saucepan. Bring to a boil, stirring constantly. Stir in the milk. Return to a boil, stirring constantly. Remove from the heat. Add the confectioners' sugar and vanilla and beat with a wooden spoon until smooth.

To assemble, spread the icing immediately between the layers and over the top and side of the cake. Sprinkle the top of the cake with the pecans. Reheat the icing over low heat if it hardens before or during spreading, stirring until soft.

SERVES 12

Carrot Cake with Cream Cheese Frosting

Cake

1 1/2 cups all-purpose flour
1 1/2 cups granulated sugar
1 teaspoon baking powder
1 teaspoon salt
1/2 teaspoon baking soda
1/2 teaspoon ground cinnamon
1/2 teaspoon ground ginger
1/2 teaspoon grated nutmeg
3/4 cup vegetable oil

1 cup mashed cooked carrots,
   at room temperature
1 (8-ounce) can crushed pineapple,
   drained
3 eggs
1 tablespoon hot water
1/2 cup (heaping) chopped walnuts
1/4 cup raisins

Cream Cheese Frosting

4 ounces cream cheese, softened
1/4 cup (1/2 stick) butter, softened

8 ounces confectioners' sugar
   (1 3/4 to 2 cups)

For the cake, preheat the oven to 350 degrees. Combine the flour, granulated sugar, baking powder, salt, baking soda, cinnamon, ginger and nutmeg in a mixing bowl and mix well. Combine the oil, carrots, pineapple, eggs and water in a bowl and mix well. Add to the flour mixture and mix until smooth. Stir in the walnuts and raisins. Pour into a greased and floured 9-inch round cake pan. Bake for 45 minutes or until the cake springs back when lightly touched. Remove to a wire rack to cool.

For the frosting, beat the cream cheese and butter in a mixing bowl until fluffy. Beat in the confectioners' sugar gradually. Spread over the top and side of the cake.

SERVES 8

Chocolate Chip Bundt Cake

1 (2-layer) package yellow cake mix
1 small package chocolate instant
    pudding mix
1/2 cup water

1/2 cup vegetable oil
3 eggs
1 cup sour cream
1 cup (6 ounces) milk chocolate chips

Preheat the oven to 350 degrees. Combine the cake mix, pudding mix, water, oil, eggs and sour cream in the order listed in a mixing bowl, beating well after each addition. Stir in the chocolate chips. Pour into a greased and floured bundt pan. Bake for 1 hour or until the cake tests done. Cool in the pan for 20 minutes. Invert onto a serving plate.

SERVES 10 TO 12

Chocolate Explosion

2 cups chopped pecans
1 small can shredded coconut
1 (2-layer) package devil's food
    cake mix

1/2 cup (1 stick) butter, softened
8 ounces cream cheese, softened
1 (1-pound) package
    confectioners' sugar

Preheat the oven to 350 degrees. Combine the pecans and coconut in a bowl. Spread in a greased 9×13-inch cake pan. Prepare the cake mix using the package directions. Pour over the pecan mixture. Cream the butter and cream cheese in a mixing bowl. Beat in the confectioners' sugar gradually. Drop by tablespoonfuls over the cake batter. (Do not spread.) Place the pan on a baking sheet to collect any spillage. Bake for 45 minutes or until a wooden pick inserted in the center comes out clean. Cool completely on a wire rack before serving.

SERVES 12 TO 15

Holiday Cake

Cake
1 cup (2 sticks) butter, softened
2 cups sugar
4 eggs
4 cups sifted all-purpose flour
1 teaspoon baking soda

1/2 teaspoon salt
1 1/2 cups buttermilk
1 cup chopped pecans
1 (8-ounce) package chopped dates
1 tablespoon grated orange zest

Orange Glaze
1/2 cup orange juice
1 cup sugar

2 tablespoons grated
orange zest

For the cake, preheat the oven to 325 degrees. Cream the butter and sugar in a mixing bowl until light and fluffy. Add the eggs 1 at a time, mixing well after each addition. Sift the flour, baking soda and salt together. Add to the creamed mixture alternately with the buttermilk, mixing well after each addition. Stir in the pecans, dates and orange zest. Pour into a greased and floured tube pan. Bake for 1 1/2 hours or until the cake tests done. Leave the cake in the pan while making the glaze.

For the glaze, combine the orange juice, sugar and orange zest in a saucepan. Cook over low heat until the sugar is dissolved, stirring constantly. Punch holes over the surface of the warm cake and separate the cake from the side of the pan. Pour the glaze over the top and down the side. Cool in the pan for several hours to overnight. Invert onto a serving plate.

SERVES 15

Italian Cream Cake with Vanilla Cream Cheese Frosting

Cake
1/2 cup (1 stick) butter, softened
1/2 cup shortening
2 cups granulated sugar
5 egg yolks
2 cups all-purpose flour
1 teaspoon baking soda

1 cup buttermilk
1 teaspoon vanilla extract
1 cup chopped pecans
1 cup shredded coconut
5 egg whites, at room temperature

Vanilla Cream Cheese Frosting
1/4 cup (1/2 stick) butter, softened
8 ounces cream cheese, softened

1 teaspoon vanilla extract
1 (1-pound) package confectioners' sugar

For the cake, preheat the oven to 350 degrees. Cream the butter, shortening and granulated sugar in a mixing bowl until light and fluffy. Add the egg yolks 1 at a time, mixing well after each addition. Sift the flour and baking soda together in a small bowl and add to the creamed mixture. Add the buttermilk and vanilla and beat until smooth and creamy. Stir in the pecans and coconut. Beat the egg whites in a mixing bowl until stiff peaks form. Fold into the batter. Pour into 3 greased and floured 9-inch round cake pans. Bake for 30 minutes or until the layers test done. Remove to wire racks to cool.

For the frosting, cream the butter and cream cheese in a mixing bowl. Beat in the vanilla and confectioners' sugar until smooth.

To assemble, spread the frosting between the layers and over the top and side of the cake.

SERVES 10 TO 12

Millionaire Cake

1 (2-layer) package chocolate cake mix
1 (14-ounce) package caramels,
  unwrapped
1 (14-ounce) can sweetened
  condensed milk

1/2 cup (1 stick) butter
2 cups chopped pecans
2 cups (12 ounces) semisweet
  chocolate chips

Preheat the oven to 350 degrees. Prepare the cake mix using the package directions. Pour 1/2 of the batter into a greased 9×13-inch cake pan. Bake for 15 minutes. Melt the caramels with the sweetened condensed milk and butter in a saucepan over low heat, stirring constantly. Pour over the cake layer. Sprinkle the pecans over the caramel mixture. Pour the remaining cake batter over the pecans. Top with the chocolate chips. Bake for 20 minutes longer. Cool in the pan before serving.

SERVE 4 TO 6

Spiced Pumpkin Cake

2 cups all-purpose flour
2 cups granulated sugar
2 teaspoons baking powder
1 teaspoon baking soda
1/2 teaspoon salt
1 teaspoon ground cinnamon
1/2 teaspoon ground cloves
1/4 teaspoon grated nutmeg

1/4 teaspoon ground ginger
4 eggs
1 (15-ounce) can pumpkin
1 cup vegetable oil
1 cup wheat bran cereal
1 cup (6 ounces) semisweet
  chocolate chips
1/2 cup confectioners' sugar

Preheat the oven to 350 degrees. Combine the flour, granulated sugar, baking powder, baking soda, salt, cinnamon, cloves, nutmeg and ginger in a large mixing bowl and mix well. Beat the eggs in a mixing bowl until foamy. Add the pumpkin, oil and cereal and mix well. Add to the flour mixture and stir just until mixed. Stir in the chocolate chips. Pour into a greased and floured bundt pan. Bake for 1 hour or until a wooden pick inserted in the center comes out clean. Cool in the pan for 15 minutes. Invert onto a serving plate. Cool completely. Sift the confectioners' sugar over the cake.

SERVES 10

Red Velvet Cake with Cream Cheese Pecan Frosting

Cake
3 1/2 cups all-purpose flour
1 teaspoon baking soda
1 teaspoon salt
2 cups granulated sugar
2 cups vegetable oil
2 eggs

1 (1-ounce) bottle red food coloring
1 teaspoon vinegar
1 teaspoon baking cocoa
1 cup buttermilk
1 teaspoon vanilla extract

Cream Cheese Pecan Frosting
1/2 cup (1 stick) butter, softened
8 ounces cream cheese, softened
1 teaspoon vanilla extract

1 (1-pound) package confectioners' sugar
1 cup pecans, chopped

For the cake, preheat the oven to 350 degrees. Mix the flour, baking soda and salt together. Combine the granulated sugar and oil in a mixing bowl and mix well. Add the eggs 1 at a time, mixing well after each addition. Combine the food coloring, vinegar and baking cocoa in a small bowl. Add to the sugar mixture and stir until mixed. Add the flour mixture alternately with the buttermilk, mixing well after each addition. Stir in the vanilla. Pour into 3 greased and floured 10-inch round cake pans. Bake for 25 to 30 minutes or until the layers test done. Remove to wire racks to cool.

For the frosting, cream the butter and cream cheese in a mixing bowl. Add the vanilla. Beat in the confectioners' sugar gradually. Fold in the pecans.

To assemble, spread the frosting between the layers and over the top and side of the cake.

SERVES 8 TO 10

Strawberry Shortcake Cake

1 (2-layer) package white cake mix
1/2 quart strawberries, chopped
1/2 cup sugar
1 cup whipping cream

2 to 3 tablespoons sugar
1 quart strawberries, cut into
    halves or quarters

Prepare and bake the cake using the package directions for two 9-inch round cake pans or two 9×9-inch cake pans. Combine 1/2 quart strawberries and 1/2 cup sugar in a bowl and mix well. Mash the strawberries in the sugar if desired. Combine the cream and 2 to 3 tablespoons sugar in a mixing bowl and beat until soft peaks form.

To assemble, place 1 cake layer on a serving plate. Spread 1/2 of the whipped cream over the top. Top with a layer of strawberry halves. Repeat the layers. Store the cake in the refrigerator. Top individual servings with the sweetened strawberries.

SERVES 12 TO 15

Marbled Syrup Cake

8 ounces light or fat-free
   cream cheese, softened
1/4 cup sugar
3 eggs
1/2 cup shortening
1 1/2 cups cane syrup or molasses
2 1/2 cups all-purpose flour

2 teaspoons ground ginger
1 teaspoon ground cinnamon
1 teaspoon ground allspice
1/4 teaspoon salt
1 1/4 teaspoons baking soda
1 cup boiling water

Preheat the oven to 350 degrees. Combine the cream cheese, sugar and 1 of the eggs in a small mixing bowl and beat until smooth. Cream the shortening and cane syrup in a mixing bowl. Add the remaining 2 eggs 1 at a time, mixing well after each addition. Mix the flour, ginger, cinnamon, allspice and salt in a large bowl. Add the cane syrup mixture and mix well. Dissolve the baking soda in the water and add to the batter. Beat until smooth but do not overmix. Pour 1/2 of the batter into a 9×13-inch cake pan coated with nonstick baking spray and flour. Pour the cream cheese mixture slowly over the batter, moving in a ribbonlike pattern from side to side. Pour the remaining batter over the top. Swirl the batter with a knife, creating a marble effect. Bake for 30 minutes or until the cake pulls away from the side of the pan.

MAKES 12 LARGE OR 24 SNACK-SIZE SERVINGS

Cane Syrup

As autumn approaches, South Louisiana's bountiful sugar cane fields are ready for harvesting. Fortunately, some of that crop heads to the syrup mill for the production of cane syrup. Enjoyed in homes and restaurants, the dark, rich syrup is a local favorite on hot biscuits or pancakes, or with a slice of French bread. It also serves as a flavorful glaze for duck or pork. New to cane syrup? Old-fashioned Marbled Syrup Cake is the perfect introduction.

Bourbon Balls

3 cups finely crushed vanilla wafers
1 cup finely ground pecans
1 cup confectioners' sugar
3 tablespoons light corn syrup

1/4 cup orange juice
1/4 cup bourbon
Confectioners' sugar for rolling

Combine the vanilla wafers, pecans, confectioners' sugar, corn syrup, orange juice and bourbon in a mixing bowl and mix well. Shape into 1-inch balls. Roll each ball in confectioners' sugar. Store in an airtight container.

Variation: For Rum Balls, simply substitute an equal amount of rum for the bourbon. If you prefer less alcohol, decrease the bourbon or rum to 2 tablespoons and increase the orange juice to 6 tablespoons.

MAKES 3 DOZEN

Almond Rocka Candy

2 cups (4 sticks) butter
1 (1-pound) package superfine sugar
2 cups slivered almonds, lightly toasted

1 (8-ounce) plain milk chocolate bar, broken into squares
1/2 cup finely chopped pecans

Combine the butter and sugar in a heavy 3-quart saucepan. Cook over medium heat for 10 minutes or until the mixture loses its bright yellow color, stirring vigorously with a wooden spoon. Stir in the almonds. Cook for 20 minutes or until the almonds are light brown and the mixture is a rich tan color, stirring constantly. Spread evenly in a greased 10×15-inch pan. Let stand for 15 minutes or until a hard film forms on the candy. Place the chocolate squares over the surface of the candy. Let stand until the chocolate softens and spread over the top using the back of a wooden spoon. Sprinkle with the pecans. Cool completely. Break into bite-size pieces. Store in an airtight container at room temperature.

MAKES ABOUT 2 POUNDS

No Occasion Needed

Everyone enjoys a kind gesture, especially if there is no special occasion. Candies, such as Almond Rocka, provide a perfect "happy" for neighbors and friends. Since it is the thought that counts, include just a few pieces of your candy in a colorful cellophane square or small gift bag. Tie with wired satin ribbon or raffia suited to the moment. Let the children contribute—using crayons or stamps and ink pads to convey an informal note of appreciation.

Peanut Butter Cups

1 pack of graham crackers,
  finely crushed
1 cup (2 sticks) butter, softened
1 cup extra-crunchy peanut butter

1 (1-pound) package
  confectioners' sugar
2 cups (12 ounces) semisweet
  chocolate chips

Combine the graham crackers, butter, peanut butter and confectioners' sugar in a bowl and mix well. Press into the bottom of a 9×13-inch pan. Melt the chocolate chips in a saucepan over very low heat. Pour over the graham cracker layer and spread into an even layer. Let stand until firm. Cut into squares.

MAKES 1 DOZEN

Pralines

2 cups sugar
1 cup buttermilk
1 teaspoon baking soda

Pinch of salt
1¼ cups chopped pecans
3 tablespoons butter

Combine the sugar, buttermilk, baking soda and salt in a saucepan and mix well. Bring to a boil. Cook over high heat for 5 minutes. Stir in the pecans and butter. Reduce the heat and stir the mixture. Cook for 5 to 10 minutes or to 234 to 240 degrees on a candy thermometer, soft-ball stage. Remove from the heat and let stand for a few minutes. Beat until the mixture thickens and begins to lose its luster. Pour by spoonfuls onto waxed paper. Let stand until cool.

MAKES 25 TO 30

Touchdown Trail Mix

1 cup (6 ounces) semisweet
  chocolate chips
1/4 cup crunchy peanut butter
1/2 cup dry-roasted peanuts

2 cups rice Chex cereal
2 cups corn Chex cereal
2 cups wheat Chex cereal
1 cup confectioners' sugar

Place the chocolate chips in a microwave-safe bowl. Microwave on High for 1½ minutes or until the chocolate is melted, stirring after 1 minute. Add the peanut butter and peanuts and stir until mixed. Fold in the Chex cereals gently, stirring until well coated. Place the confectioners' sugar in a large paper bag. Add the coated cereal. Close the bag and shake gently to coat the cereal with the confectioners' sugar. Store in an airtight container in the refrigerator.

MAKES 8 CUPS

Kahlúa Fudge Brownies

2/3 cup butter
3 (1-ounce) squares
  unsweetened chocolate
3 eggs
2 cups sugar

1/4 cup Kahlúa
1½ cups all-purpose flour
1/2 teaspoon baking powder
1/2 teaspoon salt

Preheat the oven to 350 degrees. Combine the butter and chocolate in a microwave-safe bowl. Microwave on Low until melted, stirring frequently. Combine the eggs and sugar in a mixing bowl and mix well. Stir in the chocolate mixture. Add the Kahlúa. Add the flour, baking powder and salt and mix well. Pour into a greased 10×13-inch baking pan. Bake for 23 minutes. (Do not overcook; the center should be moist.) Cool on a wire rack. Cut into squares.

SERVES 12 TO 15

Pecan Pie Brownies

1 (2-layer) package yellow cake mix
1 egg
1 cup (2 sticks) butter, softened
1/2 cup packed brown sugar

1/2 cup dark corn syrup
3 eggs
1 teaspoon vanilla extract
2 cups pecan pieces

Preheat the oven to 350 degrees. Reserve 3/4 cup of the cake mix. Combine the remaining cake mix and 1 egg in a mixing bowl and beat until smooth. Add the butter and mix well. Press onto the bottom of a 9×13-inch baking pan. Bake for 15 minutes. Combine the brown sugar, corn syrup, 3 eggs, vanilla, pecans and the reserved cake mix in a bowl and mix well. Pour over the baked layer. Bake for 25 to 30 minutes or until the brownies test done. Cool on a wire rack. Cut into squares.

SERVES 12 TO 15

Turtle Brownies

1 package brownie mix
1 (14-ounce) package caramels,
    unwrapped
1/4 cup evaporated milk

1 cup pecans, coarsely chopped
1 cup (6 ounces) semisweet
    chocolate chips

Prepare and bake the brownie mix using the package directions. Place the caramels and evaporated milk in a microwave-safe bowl. Microwave until smooth and syrupy, stirring at 45-second intervals. Sprinkle the pecans and chocolate chips over the warm brownies. Drizzle the caramel syrup over the top. Cool completely. Cut into 1- to 2-inch squares.

SERVES 8 TO 10

Chocolate Chip Pecan Pie Bars

1¹/2 cups all-purpose flour
2 tablespoons packed brown sugar
¹/2 cup (1 stick) butter
2 eggs, lightly beaten
¹/2 cup dark corn syrup
¹/2 cup packed brown sugar
¹/2 cup chopped pecans

2 tablespoons butter, melted
1 teaspoon vanilla extract
¹/4 teaspoon salt
1 cup (6 ounces) semisweet
    chocolate chips
¹/2 cup shredded coconut (optional)

Preheat the oven to 350 degrees. Combine the flour and 2 tablespoons brown sugar in a mixing bowl. Cut in ¹/2 cup butter until crumbly. Press into an ungreased 7×11-inch baking pan. Bake for 15 minutes. Combine the eggs, corn syrup, ¹/2 cup brown sugar, pecans, 2 tablespoons butter, vanilla, salt, chocolate chips and coconut in a mixing bowl and mix well. Pour over the baked layer. Bake for 25 minutes or until set. Cool until the pecan layer is firm. Cut into bars.

MAKES 32

Dark Chocolate Cookies

1 cup all-purpose flour
2/3 cup baking cocoa
1 teaspoon baking soda
¹/4 teaspoon baking powder
¹/4 teaspoon salt

1¹/4 cups sugar
3/4 cup (1¹/2 sticks) butter, softened
2 tablespoons corn syrup
1 egg
Sugar for coating

Sift the flour, baking cocoa, baking soda, baking powder and salt together. Combine the sugar, butter, corn syrup and egg in a mixing bowl and beat until fluffy. Add the flour mixture slowly and mix well. Shape into ¹/2-inch balls. Roll in sugar. Place 2 inches apart on a parchment-lined cookie sheet. Chill in the refrigerator for 20 minutes. Preheat the oven to 375 degrees. Bake for 12 to 14 minutes. (The middle should still be soft.) Cool on a wire rack. Serve the cookies with iced coffee.

SERVES 20

An Easy Cleanup

Lining baking sheets with parchment paper ensures that cakes and cookies, including these Dark Chocolate Cookies, neither burn on the bottom nor stick to the sheet. Parchment paper also eases transfer from the baking sheet to the cooling rack and makes post-baking cleaning tasks a breeze, leaving you with more time to enjoy your creations.

Graham Cracker Delight

10 to 12 whole graham crackers
1 cup (2 sticks) butter
1 cup packed light brown sugar

1 cup chopped pecans or
   slivered almonds

Preheat the oven to 350 degrees. Place the graham crackers on a foil-lined cookie sheet, keeping the crackers close together. Combine the butter, brown sugar and pecans in a saucepan. Cook over low heat for 4 to 5 minutes. Pour over the graham crackers. Bake for 10 minutes. Cool for 5 minutes. Cut into desired size with a pizza cutter.

SERVES 8

Praline Cookies

Cookie Dough
1/2 cup (1 stick) butter, softened
3/4 cup packed light brown sugar
1 egg
1 tablespoon orange juice

1/2 to 1 teaspoon orange zest (optional)
1/2 teaspoon vanilla extract
2 cups all-purpose flour
1/4 teaspoon baking soda

Pecan Filling
1 cup chopped pecans
1/2 cup packed light brown sugar
1/4 teaspoon ground cinnamon

1/4 teaspoon vanilla extract
3 to 4 tablespoons sour cream

For the cookie dough, cream the butter and brown sugar in a bowl until light and fluffy. Add the egg and mix well. Stir in the orange juice, orange zest and vanilla. Sift the flour with the baking soda. Add to the creamed mixture 1/2 cup at a time, mixing just until blended after each addition. Chill, covered, for at least 45 minutes.

For the filling, combine the pecans, brown sugar, cinnamon and vanilla in a bowl and mix well. Add enough of the sour cream to moisten the filling.

To shape the cookies and bake, preheat the oven to 350 degrees. Shape the cookie dough into 36 to 38 small balls. Place the balls on 2 nonstick cookie sheets. Make an indentation in each cookie with the end of a wooden spoon. Fill each indentation with 1/2 teaspoon of the filling. Bake for 15 minutes or until golden brown. Cool on the cookie sheets for 1 to 2 minutes. Remove to a wire rack to cool completely.

MAKES 36 TO 38

Lace Cookies

3/4 cup sugar
6 tablespoons all-purpose flour
1/4 teaspoon baking powder
1 cup quick-cooking rolled oats

1/2 cup (1 stick) butter, melted
1 egg, beaten
1 teaspoon vanilla extract

Preheat the oven to 375 degrees. Combine the sugar, flour, baking powder, rolled oats, butter, egg and vanilla in a mixing bowl and mix well. Drop by 1/2 teaspoonfuls 2 inches apart onto a foil-lined cookie sheet. Bake for 12 minutes or until the cookies are golden brown. Cool on the foil.

MAKES 3 DOZEN

Awesome Oatmeal Cookies

3/4 cup packed brown sugar
3/4 cup (1 1/2 sticks) unsalted
   butter, softened
1 1/4 cups rolled oats
1 egg
3 tablespoons milk
1 cup all-purpose flour

1/4 teaspoon baking soda
1 teaspoon ground cinnamon
1/2 teaspoon ground cloves
1/4 teaspoon salt
1/2 cup chopped walnuts
1/2 cup raisins
3/4 teaspoon vanilla extract

Combine the brown sugar, butter, rolled oats, egg, milk, flour, baking soda, cinnamon, cloves and salt in a mixing bowl and mix well. Stir in the walnuts, raisins and vanilla. Drop by tablespoonfuls 1 1/2 inches apart on a cookie sheet. Bake for 8 to 10 minutes. Cool on a wire rack for 10 minutes. Store in an airtight container.

MAKES ABOUT 2 DOZEN

The Cookie Exchange

If invited to a cookie exchange, do not mistakenly arrive empty-handed. The cookie exchange is a get-together where guests are expected to arrive with a designated number of cookies made from a chosen recipe. Guests then sample the cookies and leave with a recipe or two. Awesome Oatmeal Cookies are an old-fashioned variety that is sure to be a hit at such a gathering.

Scotch Shortbread

1 cup (2 sticks) butter, softened
1/2 cup confectioners' sugar, sifted

2 1/2 cups sifted all-purpose flour
1 teaspoon almond extract

Cream the butter and confectioners' sugar in a mixing bowl until light and fluffy. Add the flour and almond extract and mix until crumbly. Press the crumbly mixture into a 7×11-inch baking pan lined with foil and coated with nonstick baking spray. Chill, covered, for 8 to 10 hours. Preheat the oven to 300 degrees. Bake for 45 minutes. Cut the warm shortbread into small squares and prick with the tines of a fork. Cool for at least 45 minutes.

MAKES 2 DOZEN SMALL SQUARES

Wedding Cookies

1 cup (2 sticks) butter, softened
1/2 cup confectioners' sugar
1 teaspoon vanilla extract

2 cups all-purpose flour
1/4 cup finely chopped walnuts or pecans
1 cup confectioners' sugar

Preheat the oven to 400 degrees. Cream the butter, 1/2 cup confectioners' sugar and vanilla in a mixing bowl until light and fluffy. Add the flour, stirring until the mixture holds together. Add the walnuts. Shape into small balls. Place on an ungreased cookie sheet. Bake for 10 minutes. (Do not brown.) Roll the hot cookies in 1 cup confectioners' sugar. Cool completely. Roll again in the remaining confectioners' sugar.

MAKES 4 DOZEN

Blackberry Pie with Double-Crust Pastry

Double-Crust Pastry

2 cups sifted all-purpose flour
1 tablespoon sugar
1/2 teaspoon salt
1/3 cup plus 1 tablespoon shortening

1/3 cup plus 1 tablespoon cold butter,
   cut in small pieces
4 1/2 tablespoons cold milk
1 tablespoon butter, melted

Pie

5 mounded cups blackberries
1/2 cup all-purpose flour
1 to 1 1/4 cups sugar (amount depends
   on tartness of the berries)
1/2 teaspoon vanilla extract
1/4 to 1/2 teaspoon almond extract

2 to 3 teaspoons fresh lemon juice
Melted butter
1 1/2 tablespoons cold butter
Heavy cream, or an egg-milk wash
Sugar

For the pastry, sift the flour, sugar and salt together into a mixing bowl. Cut in the shortening and cold butter until crumbly. Add the milk by tablespoonfuls, mixing with a fork and adding just enough milk to form a soft dough. Divide the dough into 2 portions, making 1 slightly larger than the other. Shape each portion into a flat round. Chill, wrapped in plastic wrap, for 1 hour in the refrigerator or 30 minutes in the freezer.

For the pie, preheat the oven to 425 degrees. Toss the blackberries with the flour, 1 to 1 1/4 cups sugar, vanilla, almond extract and lemon juice in a large bowl. Let the pastry stand at room temperature for 5 minutes before rolling. Roll the larger portion into a 12-inch circle on a lightly floured surface, rolling from the center to the outside edges. Fit into a 9-inch pie plate. Trim the pastry, leaving a 1/2-inch overhang. Brush the shell with the melted butter. Pour the blackberry mixture into the shell. Dot with the cold butter.

Roll the smaller portion of the pastry into an 11- to 11 1/2-inch circle. Place over the pie filling. Fold the bottom pastry edge over the top pastry, fluting the edge and cutting vents in the top. Brush the pastry with heavy cream and sprinkle with sugar. Cover the edge of the pie with foil to prevent burning. Place the pie in a metal moat or shallow baking pan to catch excess liquid. Bake on the lowest oven rack for 55 to 60 minutes or until golden brown and the blackberry juice is thick and bubbly, reducing the oven temperature to 375 degrees after the first 30 minutes of baking if the pie is browning too fast. Cool on a wire rack.
Serve warm.

Note: For a 10-inch double-crust pie, use 2 2/3 cups sifted all-purpose flour, 1 tablespoon plus 1 teaspoon sugar, 3/4 teaspoon salt, 1/2 cup shortening, 1/2 cup (1 stick) cold butter, cut into small pieces, 6 tablespoons cold milk, 1 tablespoon butter, melted, for the pastry. Roll the larger portion of the pastry into a 13-inch circle and the smaller portion of dough into a 12- to 12 1/2-inch circle. Increase the blackberries in the pie filling to 6 (mounded) cups.

MAKES 1 PIE

Chocolate Pecan Pie

3 eggs, beaten
1 cup dark corn syrup
1/3 cup sugar
4 ounces sweet chocolate, melted
   and cooled

2 tablespoons butter, melted
2 teaspoons vanilla extract
1 1/2 cups pecan halves, lightly salted
   and toasted
1 unbaked (9-inch) pie shell

Preheat the oven to 350 degrees. Combine the eggs, corn syrup, sugar, chocolate, butter and vanilla in a large mixing bowl and mix well. Stir in the pecans. Pour into the pie shell. Bake for 50 to 60 minutes or until a knife inserted near the edge comes out clean.

SERVES 8

Kahlúa Pecan Fudge Pie

1 cup (6 ounces) semisweet
   chocolate chips
1/3 cup Kahlúa
3 eggs, lightly beaten
1 cup light or dark corn syrup
1/2 cup packed light brown sugar
2 teaspoons vanilla extract

1/4 teaspoon salt
1/4 cup (1/2 stick) butter, melted
1 1/2 cups chopped pecans
1 unbaked (9-inch) pie shell
1 cup heavy whipping cream (optional)
1 tablespoon Kahlúa (optional)

Combine the chocolate chips and 1/3 cup Kahlúa in a small saucepan. Cook over low heat until the chocolate melts, stirring until smooth. Combine the eggs, corn syrup, brown sugar, vanilla and salt in a mixing bowl and mix well. Stir in the chocolate mixture. Add the butter and 1 cup of the pecans. Pour into the pie shell. Sprinkle the remaining 1/2 cup pecans over the top. Bake for 45 to 50 minutes or until the center is barely set and the pastry is light brown. Cool on a wire rack. Combine the whipping cream and 1 tablespoon Kahlúa in a mixing bowl and beat until soft peaks form. Top each serving of pie with a dollop of the Kahlúa cream.

MAKES 1 PIE

Chocolate-Dipped Strawberries

Make Chocolate-Dipped Strawberries to accompany the Kahlúa Pecan Fudge Pie using this simple method. Rinse fresh strawberries and allow them to fully dry, approximately one to two hours. Melt a good-quality chocolate bar in a double boiler. Dip a portion of each strawberry in the chocolate. Place the berries on a baking sheet lined with waxed paper, being careful that they don't touch. Refrigerate for three to four hours. Serve the same day.

Coconut Pie

2 cups milk
3/4 cup sugar
1/2 cup baking mix
4 eggs

1/4 cup (1/2 stick) butter, melted
1 1/2 teaspoons vanilla extract
1 cup shredded coconut

Preheat the oven to 350 degrees. Combine the milk, sugar, baking mix, eggs, butter and vanilla in a blender and process for 3 minutes. Pour into a greased 9-inch pie plate. Let stand for 5 minutes. Sprinkle with the coconut. Bake for 45 minutes. Serve warm or cool.

SERVES 8

Lemon Pie

1 (14-ounce) can sweetened
    condensed milk
8 ounces cream cheese, softened

1/3 cup lemon juice
1 teaspoon vanilla extract
1 graham cracker pie shell

Combine the sweetened condensed milk, cream cheese, lemon juice and vanilla in a mixing bowl and mix until smooth and creamy. Pour into the pie shell. Chill for 8 hours. Garnish with cut fruit.

SERVES 8

Lemon Curd Tarts

3 eggs
1 cup sugar
3/4 cup (1 1/2 sticks) butter or margarine
1 tablespoon grated lemon zest

1/2 cup fresh lemon juice
24 miniature pastry shells, baked
Whipped topping or whipped cream
(optional)

Beat the eggs in a saucepan over hot water. Add the sugar, butter, lemon zest and lemon juice and mix well. Cook over hot water for 8 to 10 minutes or until the mixture coats a spoon, stirring constantly. Pour into the pastry shells. Top with whipped topping.

SERVES 24

Chocolate Amaretto Tarts

2 refrigerator 9-inch pie pastries
1 ounce unsweetened chocolate
1/2 cup (1 stick) butter, softened
2 cups confectioners' sugar
1 tablespoon vanilla extract

Dash of salt
4 egg yolks
3 tablespoons amaretto
1 1/2 cups heavy whipping cream
1 tablespoon amaretto

Prepare tart shells by cutting rounds from the pastry and fitting into muffin cups. Bake using the directions on the pastry package. Melt the chocolate in a heavy saucepan over low heat. Cream the butter in a mixing bowl. Add the confectioners' sugar gradually, beating until light and fluffy. Stir in the chocolate, vanilla and salt. Add the egg yolks 1 at a time, mixing well after each addition. Stir in 3 tablespoons amaretto 1 tablespoon at a time, mixing well after each addition. Whip the cream in a mixing bowl until soft peaks form. Add the 1 tablespoon amaretto gradually. Fold 1 cup of the whipped cream into the amaretto mixture. Spoon the amaretto filling into the cooled tart shells. Chill for 3 to 4 hours or until firm. Top each tart with a dollop of the remaining whipped cream.

Note: If you are concerned about using raw egg yolks, use yolks from eggs pasteurized in their shells, which are sold at some specialty food stores, or use an equivalent amount of pasteurized egg substitute.

MAKES 6

Whipping the Cream

Chocolate Amaretto Tarts make a lovely selection for a tea-time affair. The whipped cream necessary for the tarts should be prepared with very cold cream. For best results, also chill the bowl in which the cream will be whipped, along with the whisk or beaters that will be used. This technique will increase the volume of the whipped cream.

Southern Pecan Tart

1 refrigerator pie pastry
4 eggs, lightly beaten
1 cup packed dark brown sugar
1/4 teaspoon salt
1/2 cup light corn syrup

3 tablespoons unsalted butter, melted
1 teaspoon vanilla extract
1 1/2 cups chopped pecans
1 1/4 cups perfect pecan halves

Preheat the oven to 325 degrees. Unfold the pastry into a 10-inch tart pan with a removable bottom. Fit the pastry into the pan and trim the edge. Combine the eggs, brown sugar, salt and corn syrup in a mixing bowl and mix well. Add the melted butter and vanilla and stir until smooth. Stir in the chopped pecans. Pour into the tart shell. Arrange the pecan halves neatly in rows across the filling. Bake for 45 to 50 minutes or until the pastry is lightly browned and the filling is set. Cool completely on a wire rack. Remove the tart from the pan and let stand for 1 hour longer before cutting.

SERVES 10

A Refined Classic

Those with pecan trees make their way outside with buckets and bags in hand when Louisiana pecans begin falling to the ground in autumn. Once shelled and cleaned, the gems are used throughout the winter in countless dishes and desserts. For a special occasion or the holiday table, Southern Pecan Tart is a refined take on the traditional pecan pie. Arrange the pecan halves with tidy precision for an especially beautiful presentation.

Autumn Apple Buckle

Crumb Topping

1 1/2 cups all-purpose flour
3/4 cup packed brown sugar
1 teaspoon cinnamon
3/4 teaspoon finely grated lemon zest

Pinch of salt
1/2 cup (1 stick) plus 1 tablespoon
   unsalted butter, softened
1/2 cup coarsely chopped walnuts

Apple Buckle

2 cups all-purpose flour
2 teaspoons baking powder
1/4 teaspoon ground ginger
1/4 teaspoon salt
3/4 cup (1 1/2 sticks) unsalted butter,
   softened
1/2 cup granulated sugar

1/4 cup honey
2 eggs
1 teaspoon finely grated lemon zest
1 teaspoon vanilla extract
1/2 cup half-and-half
2 pounds Granny Smith apples peeled,
   cored and cut into 1/2-inch cubes

Sweetened Sour Cream

1 cup sour cream

2 tablespoons brown sugar

For the crumb topping, combine the flour, brown sugar, cinnamon, lemon zest and salt in a food processor and pulse 2 or 3 times. Add the butter and process until crumbly. Add the walnuts and pulse 3 times. Remove to a bowl and press the mixture to form large crumbs.

For the apple buckle, preheat the oven to 350 degrees. Combine the flour, baking powder, ginger and salt in a bowl and mix well. Beat the butter in a mixing bowl until creamy. Add the granulated sugar. Beat for 3 minutes or until light and fluffy. Add the honey and mix well. Add the eggs, lemon zest and vanilla and beat until smooth. Add the flour mixture alternately with the half-and-half, mixing well after each addition. Fold in the apples. Spoon the batter into a buttered and floured 10-inch springform pan and smooth the top. Sprinkle with the crumb topping. Bake for 1 1/4 hours or until the topping is golden and a wooden pick inserted in the center comes out clean. Cool in the pan for at least 1 hour. Remove the side of the pan.

For the sweetened sour cream, combine the sour cream and brown sugar in a bowl and mix well. Serve with wedges of the apple buckle.

SERVES 10 TO 12

Baklava

Pecan Filling
6 cups coarsely chopped pecans
2 cups sugar

2 teaspoons vanilla extract
1/2 cup water

Syrup
3 cups sugar
1^{1}/2 cups water

1^{1}/2 teaspoons vanilla extract
1^{1}/2 teaspoons lemon juice

Pastry
2 (1-pound) packages phyllo dough,
   thawed

2^{1}/2 cups (5 sticks) unsalted butter,
   melted

For the pecan filling, combine the pecans, sugar, vanilla and water in a large bowl and stir well.

For the syrup, combine the sugar and water in a small saucepan. Bring to a boil. Reduce the heat to medium. Cook for 5 minutes. Add the vanilla and lemon juice. Cook for 5 minutes longer. Remove from the heat and let the syrup cool.

For the pastry, preheat the oven to 350 degrees. Unroll 1 package of the phyllo dough and cover it with waxed paper topped with a damp towel. Keep the unused portion covered until needed. Place 1 sheet of the dough in a buttered 9×13-inch baking pan. Brush with melted butter. Trim any excess dough from the side of the pan or fold the dough into the pan, folding alternating sides with each layer. Layer the remaining dough (25 to 30 layers) in the pan, brushing each sheet except the top one with melted butter. Spread the pecan filling over the top layer. Unroll the remaining package of phyllo dough and cover it with waxed paper topped with a damp towel. Repeat the layering and buttering (25 to 30 layers), ending with butter on the top layer of phyllo. Cut into diamond or square pieces, using a very sharp knife. Bake for 40 to 45 minutes or until golden brown.

To finish the baklava, spoon just enough of the cooled syrup over the hot baklava to cover but not saturate the pieces. Cool for several hours. Remove from the pan. Store in cookie tins for several weeks. (To retain crispness, do not use plastic containers.)

MAKES ABOUT 3 DOZEN

Coconut Bread Pudding

Pudding

8 slices bread, torn into pieces
4 cups warm milk
4 egg yolks
1 egg white
1 1/2 cups sugar

1 (5-ounce) can evaporated milk
1 tablespoon almond extract
1 1/4 cups shredded coconut
1/4 cup (1/2 stick) butter, melted

Meringue

3 egg whites, at room temperature
6 tablespoons sugar

1 tablespoon almond extract
1/4 cup shredded coconut

For the pudding, preheat the oven to 300 degrees. Soak the bread in the warm milk in a large bowl. Combine the egg yolks and egg white in a mixing bowl and beat lightly. Add the sugar, evaporated milk and almond extract gradually, mixing well after each addition. Add to the bread mixture and mix well. Stir in the coconut and butter. Pour into a buttered 9×13-inch baking pan. Bake for 1 hour and 10 minutes or until a spatula inserted in the center comes out clean.

For the meringue, increase the oven temperature to 325 degrees. Beat the egg whites in a mixing bowl until soft peaks form. Add the sugar gradually, beating until stiff peaks form. Beat in the almond extract. Spread the meringue over the pudding, sealing to the edge. Sprinkle with the coconut. Bake for 5 to 7 minutes or until the meringue is beginning to brown.

SERVES 8 TO 10

No Sauce Required

This old-fashioned Coconut Bread Pudding is a coconut lover's delight. Due to its rich, moist texture, there is no need for a sauce on the side, as with many bread puddings. For a flavorful variation, substitute dense French bread or buttery brioche as your bread of choice. Be sure that every morsel is adequately soaked in the rich liquid before baking. Doubling the meringue is a tasty and attractive touch as well.

Blueberry Cheesecake

Crumb Crust
1 (12-ounce) package vanilla wafer
  cookies, finely crushed

3/4 cup (1 1/2 sticks) butter, melted

Filling
40 ounces cream cheese, softened
1 1/4 cups sugar
6 eggs
2 egg yolks

2 1/2 tablespoons all-purpose flour
2 1/2 teaspoons vanilla extract
1/4 cup heavy cream

Topping
3 tablespoons cornstarch
3 tablespoons water
1 cup sugar
1 cup water

2 1/2 cups fresh blueberries, or
  1 (16-ounce) package frozen
  unsweetened blueberries, thawed
  and drained

For the crumb crust, Combine the vanilla wafer crumbs and butter in a bowl and mix well. Press onto the bottom and 2 inches up the side of a greased 9-inch springform pan. Chill, covered, while making the filling.

For the filling, beat the cream cheese in a mixing bowl for 25 minutes, adding 8 ounces to the bowl at a time. Add the sugar. Beat for 5 minutes. Add the eggs and egg yolks 1 at a time, beating for 2 minutes after each addition. Add the flour and vanilla and mix well. Beat in the cream.

To assemble and bake, preheat the oven to 500 degrees. Pour the filling into the prepared crumb crust. Bake for 10 minutes. Reduce the heat to 200 degrees. Bake for 1 hour. Turn off the oven and let stand for 1 hour without opening the oven door. Cool completely on a wire rack.

For the topping, combine the cornstarch and 3 tablespoons water in a small bowl and stir until smooth. Combine the sugar and 1 cup water in a saucepan. Cook over medium heat until the sugar dissolves, stirring constantly. Stir in the cornstarch mixture. Bring to a boil, stirring constantly until thickened. Removed from the heat and let cool. Stir in the blueberries. Spoon over the cooled cheesecake. Chill, loosely covered, until serving time.

SERVES 16 TO 20

To Your Taste

Blueberry topping on a cheesecake is a classic combination, but everyone has his or her flavor preferences. Using this rich cheesecake as a base, creative cooks can easily concoct countless variations. Try substituting other frozen fruits, such as strawberries or raspberries. For a nonfruit option, omit the blueberry topping and drizzle the basic cheesecake with caramel and melted chocolate, then sprinkle with chopped toasted pecans.

Pumpkin Cheesecake with Gingersnap Crust

Gingersnap Crust
1 1/2 cups gingersnap cookies, crushed
3 tablespoons packed brown sugar

6 tablespoons butter, melted

Filling
24 ounces cream cheese, softened
1 cup packed brown sugar
1 1/2 cups canned pumpkin
1/2 cup heavy cream
1/3 cup maple syrup

1 tablespoon vanilla extract
1 teaspoon ground cinnamon
1/2 teaspoon ground allspice
4 eggs

For the gingersnap crust, combine the gingersnap crumbs, brown sugar and butter in a bowl and mix well. Press onto the bottom and 2 inches up the side of a greased and floured 9-inch springform pan.

For the filling, beat the cream cheese and brown sugar in a mixing bowl until light and fluffy. Stir in the pumpkin. Add the cream, maple syrup, vanilla, cinnamon and allspice and mix well. Add the eggs 1 at a time, beating well after each addition.

To assemble and bake, preheat the oven to 325 degrees. Pour the filling into the prepared crust. Bake for 1 1/2 hours or until the center is set. Cool in the pan for 30 minutes. Chill for 8 to 10 hours before serving.

SERVES 8

Chocolate Chip Cream Cheese Ball

1/2 cup (1 stick) butter, softened
8 ounces cream cheese, softened
1/4 teaspoon vanilla extract
3/4 cup confectioners' sugar

2 tablespoons packed brown sugar
3/4 cup miniature semisweet
   chocolate chips
3/4 cups finely chopped pecans

Cream the butter, cream cheese and vanilla in a mixing bowl until light and fluffy. Add the confectioners' sugar and brown sugar gradually, beating just until smooth. Stir in the chocolate chips. Chill, covered, for 2 hours. Shape into a ball on a large piece of plastic wrap. Cover with the plastic wrap and chill for 1 hour longer. Roll the ball in the chopped pecans just before serving. Serve with regular or chocolate-flavored graham crackers.

SERVES 15 TO 20

Cinnamon Logs

1 (16-ounce) loaf thin-sliced sandwich
   bread, crusts trimmed
8 ounces cream cheese, softened
1/2 cup confectioners' sugar

1 egg white
1 cup granulated sugar
1 tablespoon ground cinnamon
1/2 cup (1 stick) butter, melted

Preheat the oven to 350 degrees. Roll the bread slices 1/4 inch thick with a rolling pin. Combine the cream cheese, confectioners' sugar and egg white in a mixing bowl and beat at medium speed until smooth. Spread each bread slice with the cream cheese mixture. Roll up the bread slices to form logs. Combine the granulated sugar and cinnamon in a shallow dish. Dip each log in the melted butter and roll in the cinnamon mixture. Place on a lightly greased baking sheet. Bake for 15 minutes.

Note: You may freeze the logs before baking and store in freezer bags in the freezer for future use.

SERVES 10 TO 12

Saucy Fruit

2 nectarines, sliced
1 pint blueberries
1 pint blackberries
1 pint strawberries, sliced
2 cups unflavored yogurt

1 1/2 cups packed dark brown sugar
2 tablespoons rum
1 teaspoon ground cinnamon
1/2 teaspoon grated nutmeg

Divide the nectarines, blueberries, blackberries and strawberries among 4 to 6 large wine or martini glasses. Whisk the yogurt and brown sugar together in a bowl. Stir in the rum, cinnamon and nutmeg. Serve over the fruit.

SERVES 4 TO 6

Ladyfingers Dessert

2 (14-ounce) cans sweetened
   condensed milk
3 1/2 cups whole milk
5 egg yolks
2 teaspoons vanilla extract

1 3/4 cups baking cocoa
2 1/2 cups water
2 (14-ounce) packages
   ladyfinger cookies
1 can whipped cream

Combine the condensed milk, whole milk, egg yolks and vanilla in a saucepan. Cook over low heat for 40 to 45 minutes or until smooth and thickened, stirring frequently. Dissolve the baking cocoa in the water in a saucepan. Cook over low heat for 15 minutes or until thick. Dip the ladyfingers in the chocolate mixture. Layer the ladyfingers and the milk mixture 1/2 at a time in a 9×13-inch baking dish. Chill for 8 to 10 hours. Cover the dessert with whipped cream before serving.

SERVES 12 TO 14

Tarte Tatin

2¹/2 tablespoons butter
2 cups sugar
3¹/2 to 3³/4 pounds Granny Smith
   apples, peeled

8 ounces frozen puff pastry dough,
   thawed

Preheat the oven to 400 degrees. Melt the butter in a saucepan over medium heat. Add the sugar. Cook until dark amber, stirring frequently. Pour into a 9-inch baking pan with sides at least 2¹/2 inches high. Let stand until cool. Cut 4 thick slices from top to bottom around the core of each apple. Arrange the apples flat side down over the cooled caramel. Bake for 50 minutes or until the apples are tender. Unfold the puff pastry using the package directions. Roll into a 9-inch circle on a lightly floured surface. Let stand, covered with plastic wrap, while the apples are baking. Prick the pastry 15 to 20 times with a fork. Place over the apples. Bake for 35 minutes or until golden brown. Cool in the pan on a wire rack for 20 to 25 minutes. Invert onto a 12- to 14-inch serving platter. Top each serving with vanilla ice cream or crème fraîche if desired.

SERVES 8

On the Side

Full of rustic charm, Tarte Tatin is a classic French dessert. As you will note in the recipe, it is actually prepared upside down. Although purists might feel that Tarte Tatin, with its melding of caramel and apple flavors, is best appreciated alone, we enjoy it topped with a scoop of vanilla ice cream, a dollop of whipped cream, or, better yet, a touch of crème fraîche.

Strawberry and Blueberry Trifle

1 (10-ounce) angel food cake, torn
  into cubes
16 ounces cream cheese, softened
1 (5-ounce) can evaporated milk
1 cup sugar

1 teaspoon vanilla extract
1 (21-ounce) can blueberry pie filling
8 ounces whipped topping
Fresh strawberries

Line the bottom of a 9×13-inch baking dish with the angel food cake cubes. Combine the cream cheese, evaporated milk, sugar and vanilla in a mixing bowl and mix well. Pour over the cake cubes. Chill for 15 minutes. Pour the pie filling over the cake mixture. Chill for 15 minutes longer. Spread the whipped topping over the layers and top with strawberries. Chill for at least 2 hours before serving.

SERVES 12

Appendix

Contributors

Martha Abshire
Ashley Alexander
Dawn Trahan Alexander
Amy Allums
Ann Landry Allums
Louise Altick
Maryan Amitai
Kenny Ancelet
Carolyn Artall
Lisa Babineaux
Marguerite Ballard
Candice Barilleaux
Sarah Beacham
Allison Bean
Jerry Belaire
Misty Bennett
Sarah Berthelot
Lauren Besse
Betsy St. Julien Billeaud
Christa Billeaud
Andy Black
Anne Black
Susan Blanchard
Rebecca Blanchet
Elise Bouchner
Jackie Bouligny
Ellen Bourg
Katherine McDonald Bourg
Jackie Giroir Bourgeois
Miriam Bourgeois
Connie Arceneaux Boustany
Leslie Brauns
Erica Bronson
David Broussard
Dot Beyt Broussard
Kim G. Broussard
Martha Broussard
Terri R. Broussard
Nicole Brown
Virginia Brown
Shelley Brumbaugh
Clarice Burch
Alicia Burleigh
Cherie Burlet
Elizabeth Cella Burnell
Darrellyn Burts
Annette Busch
Ellin Busch
Mary Michael Butcher
Blair Bowden Cabes
Anne Sonnier Calhoun
Patsy Shelton Cella
Joretta Chance
Pamela Chapman
Hazel Comeaux
Dimet Conrad
Mildred Cortez
Corinne Cotten
Theresa Cotten
Jill Cox
Penny Crawford

Charlotte Cryer
Russell Cryer
Michelle Curtis
Cherie Starks Daigle
Claire Cortez Daly
Charlotte Darby
Rhonda Darby
Shannon Seiler Dartez
Kathy Daugherty
Sandra Day
Susan Delcambre
Marie Doiron
Harold Domingue
Monica Domingue
Andrea Ducharme
Jennifer Ducharme
Katherine Dugas
Novella Dugas
Debby Duplechain
Fran Dupre
Caroline Dupuis
Jimmy Dupuis
Jimmy Dupuis, Sr.
Susan Dupuis
Deborah D. Eckholdt
Jim Farasey
Natalee Farasey
Pat Olson Ferguson
Carrie Foard
Carolyn Fontenot
Donna Forman
Mimi Francez
Robert Francez
Laurie A. Freret
Heather Fuller
Jim Fuller
Connie T. Galloway
Kay Karré Gautreaux
Monique Giroir Gideon
Al Giroir
Janet Gooch
Melanie Goudelocke
Betty Gray
Ormond Guenard
Mary K. Hamilton
Mark Hanna
Tanya Hanna
Lisa Hannie
Christina Harper
Nita Harrington
Allyson Hebert
Jane Hundley Hebert
Marci Hebert
Nanette Soileau Heggie
Heather N. Hennigan
Julie Hill
Katherine P. Hill
Kathy Hill
Alison Howard
Rachel Hughes
Kathy Hundley

Lynne Jackson
Barbara Berard Jefferson
Narcille Johnson
Tim Johnson
Angelle Judice
Karen F. Juneau
Karen P. Juneau
Wendell Juneau
Inez Boustany Karré
Judy Kennedy
Ann Kergan
Betsy Koke
Miriam Kolwe
Melanie LaFleur
Elmira Landry
Erin Landry
Amanda LaVigne
Gertrude LeBlanc
Janice LeBlanc
Marilyn Lee
Peggy A. Lee
Cally Lege
Ketha H. Lewis
Nancy Terrell Stutsman Lewis
Amber Littlefield
Debbie Mahony
Judy Mahtook
Mary Ann Mahtook
Ann Morehead Marino
Linda Marino
Kay Marix
Lesley Maxwell
Liz Maxwell
Patsy McCord
Karen V. McGlasson
Margaret Eubank McGlasson
Susan McGuire
Neil Melms
Pam Melms
Ted Menard
Monique Michot
Suzanne C. Miller
Ashley Moncla
Faith Moody
Thelma Moody
Joyce Morehead
Angela Morrison
Dawn Morvant
Bettina Mouton
Cecile Mouton
Annette Myers
Susan Myers
Becky Nash
Pat Naumann
Julie Nelson
Adele Netterville
Nanette Nolan
Ginger Norvell
Jean Ostrich
Cheryl Ottinger
Catherine Odom Pankey

Jeanette Plauché Parker
Edie Parsons
Bindu Patel
Stacy Patin
Elena Arcos Pecoraro
Mary Ann Penny
Elizabeth Picard
Susie Piccione
Valerie Poole
Mary Alice Prejean
Jennie Rader
Javier Raices
Tracy Ralston
Gathy Ryals Reed
Marcy B. Reeves
Doris Reggie
Rhonda Richard
Rosalind Moody Robertson
Karen Schmid
Marianne Schneider
Willie C. Schutz
Kelly Scofield
Marion Seemann
Angela Shields
Maggie Trahan Simar
Katheryn Simon
Elizabeth Hartiens Smith
Phern Stagg
Claudette St. Amant
Sheri Steffek
Sandy Stewart
Jeigh Stipe
Craig Storer
Pam Stroup
Melanee Tackaberry
Lucille Taliaferro
Deborah Terribile
Cynthia Devillier Thompson
Dana Belaire Topham
Denise Torian
Jackie Trahan
Tet Trahan
Elizabeth Trotter
Ann Turnbow
Roger Turner
Mary A. Usner
Betsy Vigorito
Mary Vinson
Phyllis D. Walters
Bonnie Warner
Kathy Cortez Whipp
Billie M. White
Leu Strange Wilder
Joan Williams
Allison Womble
Jan Wyatt
Noemi Wyatt
Crystall Young

Recipe Testers

Amy Aderman
Dawn Trahan Alexander
Maryan Amitai
Carolyn Artall
Lisa Babineaux
Candice Barilleaux
Dee Dee Becquet
Sarah Berthelot
Christa Billeaud
Andy Black
Anne Black
Rebecca Blanchet
Elise Bouchner
Katherine McDonald Bourg
Miriam Bourgeois
Lynn Bourque
Cherie Burlet
John Butcher
Mary Michael Butcher
Pam Capell
Elizabeth Champion
Dimet Conrad
Carolyn Crain
Evelyn Craton
Charlotte Cryer
Michelle Curtis

Pam Daniel
Rhonda Darby
Sandra Day
Andrea Ducharme
Kris Dugas
Susan Dupuis
Deborah D. Eckholdt
Sarah Firmin
Debbie Foreman
Donna Foreman
Mimi Francez
Gena Francis
Leslie Fritcher
Karen Gambel
Mary Gaston
Jaimee Gaudin
Monique Giroir Gideon
Ormond Guenard
Grace Guidry
Julie Gurzi
Craig Haydell
Gaylyn Hebert
Lisa Hebert
Marci Hebert
Heather N. Hennigan
Elizabeth Hesterly

Julie Hill
Alison Howard
Rachel Hughes
Colby Jones
Angelle Judice
Karen F. Juneau
Karen P. Juneau
Molly Kallenberger
Ann Kergan
Mary Kreuz
Cassie Landry
Erin Landry
Martha Latiolais
Gertrude LeBlanc
Margie LeBlanc
Cally Lege
Ann Marie Littell
Amber Littlefield
Debbie Mahony
Judy Mahtook
Myra Malagarie
Ann Morehead Marino
Susan McGuire
Angela Mills
Ashley Moncla
Faith Moody

Laura Moroux
Angela Morrison
Dawn Morvant
Bettina Mouton
Cecile Mouton
Julie Nelson
Nancy Northcutt
Susie Piccione
Angie Quoyeser
Shanna Ray
Lea Ann Remondet
Anne Sagrera
Karen Schmid
Maggie Trahan Simar
Katheryn Simon
Lise Anne D. Slatten
Elizabeth Hartiens Smith
Cynthia Devillier Thompson
Dana Belaire Topham
Billie M. White
Allison Womble
Noemi Wyatt
Crystall Young

Acknowledgments

Photography Props
Sarah Berthelot
Anne Black
Alicia Burleigh
Annette Busch
Cherie Burlet
Ann Butcher
Betty Butcher
Mary Michael Butcher
Katherine McDonald Bourg
Miriam Bourgeois
Charlotte Cryer
Michelle Curtis
Marla David
Sandra Day
Laura Ann Edwards
Mimi Francez
Betsy Koke
Beth Landry
Janice LeBlanc
Marilyn Lee
Judy Mahtook
Ann Morehead Marino
Angela Morrison
Stacy Patin
Susie Piccione
Allison Womble

Food Preparation
Anne Black
Miriam Bourgeois
Annette Busch
Charlotte Cryer
Rhonda Darby
Andrea Ducharme
Monique Gideon
Betsy Koke
Gertrude LeBlanc
Janice LeBlanc
Judy Mahtook
Ann Morehead Marino
Julie Nelson
Stacy Patin

Menu Development
Maryan Amitai
Anne Black
Miriam Bourgeois
Annette Busch
Michelle Curtis
Rhonda Darby
Sandra Day
Andrea Ducharme
Carolyn Fontenot
Mimi Francez
Monique Giroir Gideon
Betsy Koke
Janice LeBlanc
Judy Mahtook
Bettina Mouton
Julie Nelson

Occasional Menu Index

Index

Junior League of Lafayette Publications

Talk About Good!

The original cookbook from Cajun Country, this is a collection of time-honored recipes filled with renowned family mealtime favorites and a variety to satisfy everyone's palate. It's a seafood lover's cookbook.
McIlhenny Tabasco Community Cookbook Hall of Fame Award

Talk About Good II

Our second cookbook features authentic Cajun recipes with an unpretentious, yet exotic flair. It is adorned with twelve full-color prints by internationally acclaimed "Blue Dog" artist George Rodrigue. You will also treasure its wine reference guide, twelve special occasion menus, wild game recipes, party planning hints, and a spice and herb guide.
McIlhenny Tabasco Community Cookbook Hall of Fame Award

Tell Me More

The third Junior League of Lafayette cookbook is bursting with recipes and stories chronicling Cajun ways, past and present. You will learn to make great dishes using basic pantry items, following recipes from legendary Cajun cooks as well as those of a new generation. The book features prints by the late Floyd Sonnier, the nationally known Cajun artist.
Southern Regional Tabasco Community Cookbook Award

Something to Talk About

Occasions We Celebrate in South Louisiana

and our previous publications may be purchased from the Junior League of Lafayette at 337.988.2739 or by visiting www.juniorleagueoflafayette.com.

Proceeds from *Something to Talk About, Talk About Good! Talk About Good II,* and *Tell Me More* help provide financial support for the Junior League of Lafayette and its mission to promote voluntarism, develop the potential of women, and improve the community through the effective action and leadership of trained volunteers.